Diary of a Grammar School

King's Lynn

Michael Walker

K.E.S. Publications

King's Lynn

First published in Great Britain in 2010 by
K.E.S. Publications
King Edward VII School
Gaywood Road
King's Lynn
PE30 4ER

Typeset in Times New Roman and printed by DSD Colour Printers,
King's Lynn.

A catalogue record for this book is available from the British Library.

ISBN 978-0-956569707

Contents

Introduction

The aim of this book is to trace the development of the Lynn Grammar School from its origin in 1510 to 1903 when it was merged with the Lynn Technical School and became King Edward VII Grammar School. In my earlier book on the history of the school, *King Edward VII School, A Centenary Celebration* (2005) only the first chapter and a part of the second were devoted to the early history of the school and so the barest outline was provided. Since 2010 is the 500th Anniversary of the founding of the school I felt that the early period deserved much more serious attention.

I have drawn heavily on the entries in the King's Lynn Hall Books, the records of the Halls or meetings of the Corporation, which are preserved in the Borough Archive sited in the Old Gaol House building. In addition the records of Committee meetings, especially in the nineteenth century, and a range of other documents relating to the Grammar School have proved invaluable. Some books on the history of Lynn have relevant information and comment but coverage is brief and they do contain inaccuracies, some of which have been repeated from earlier sources.

This book takes the form of a diary of entries from the documentary evidence together with commentaries on a number of themes such as appointments of and information on the Schoolmasters and Ushers, curriculum and organisation, building and maintenance work carried out on the School and the Schoolmaster's house and on scholarships to colleges in the University of Cambridge.

In preparation for writing this book I have devoted a great deal of time to the transcribing of entries relating to the Grammar School in the Corporation Hall Books and Committee Books. The complete transcriptions are available in the Borough Archive should anyone wish to consult them and copies can be purchased from King Edward VII School. The early entries in the Hall Books are written in secretary hand and are not easy to read. Two examples, from 1534 and 1550, the first to mention the Grammar School and the Schoolmaster respectively, are reproduced as they appear in the Hall Books. An entry from the Chamberlains' Account for 1599/1600 is also reproduced. Transcriptions are provided in the text.

The problem of reading these early entries is partly the handwriting but also the fact that the letters were formed differently and that there was not one but many forms of the different letters used. In addition the spelling of words was not fixed until printing had become well established. To illustrate this point an entry from the 1577 Quit Rents transcribed by Peter Sykes is reproduced below:

> Item. The same holdeth ther in two pieces lyynge tigither conteynynge by estymacon ffyve acr of pasture late in thoccupacon of Mr Watters now in thoccupacon of [blank] lyynge in the same felde in bredethe between the lande of the dean and chapter afforsaid and the landes of the heires of Edward Watters somtyme Trewys and the landes of the said Robert Gervis. And the sowth headd abbutt upon the landes of the said Edward Watters somtyme Trewis and the landes of the deane and chapter of Christs Church Norwich afforsaid.

This source is referred to in Chapter 1 and the full reference cited. In order to make the entries more easily readable I have transcribed them into modern English and added some punctuation which is often lacking in the original. However the spelling of names has not been changed and it will be noticed that often they vary from entry to entry and even within one entry.

Also for ease of interpretation I have dated the Hall Book entries according to the modern calendar, despite the fact that until 1752 the New Year in England began on Lady Day (25 March) not 1 January. In addition dates given in the Hall Books in terms of the regnal year and saints' days have been translated into the more usual format. For example the 1534 entry referred to above is taken from the minutes of the Hall held on 'Friday after Gregory, Pope, in the 25th Henry VIII.' Since the Feast of St Gregory, which is 12 March, was a Thursday in 1534, the Friday after the feast day was 13 March. [1]

One further point of explanation concerns money. Salaries and costs are given in pre-decimal currency when there were twenty shillings to the pound and twelve pennies to the shilling. Sometimes documents refer to marks and nobles. A mark was two-thirds of a pound (13s 4d) and a noble was half a mark or a third of a pound (6s 8d). The value of one pound in the past greatly exceeded its current value but comparisons are not easy. One piece of research, available online, gives the equivalent values of the British pound going back to 1264. [2] Unfortunately different criteria give very different values. According to this source, £10, the Schoolmaster's salary in 1550, was worth in 2008 about £2500, based on the retail price index, but some £39,000 based on average earnings. The first seems too low and the other much too high. Towards the end of Chapter 2 some more meaningful comparisons are made between the costs of everyday items and wages.

Over the past five centuries the school has had an interesting but chequered history. I have enjoyed doing the research and I very much hope that readers will find the story as fascinating as I have.

Michael Walker,
King's Lynn, 2010

Acknowledgements

I should like to express my thanks to all those who have provided help and advice in the preparation of this book, in particular to Susan Maddock, Principal Archivist at the Norfolk Record Office who has given invaluable help on the transcription of early entries in the Hall Books. I am also grateful to the Norfolk Record Office for permission to reproduce the extracts from the documents in the Borough Archive.

Thanks are also due to the following: Peter Sykes for help in reading documents and for sharing the fruits of his research in the Borough Archive; Colin Barton for allowing me access to his personal resources and for help with illustrations; David Pitcher for advice on useful sources of information and photographs; Bob Booth and Steve Jukes for help with photographs; and to Tim Steer for reading the manuscript and making helpful suggestions.

A number of photographs/figures are reproduced by kind permission: Figure 3, the sketch map of land in Gaywood (Peter Sykes and Colin Barton); Figure 14, Henry Bell's sketch of the Grammar School (King's Lynn Museum); Figure 16, The Shambles on Saturday Market Place (Brian and Jan Gadd Collection); and Figures 22 and 23, the Reverend J B Slight (Judith Mooney).

Finally I should like to thank Michael Douglass, Head of King Edward VII School, and my wife, Elizabeth for their unfailing help and support.

1. 1510 and all that

Although there must have been some education provided by priests and monks in Lynn before 1510, it is this date, the date of the will of Thomas Thoresby, from which the origin of the Grammar School is traced. Thomas Thoresby was an important burgess who had been Mayor of Lynn three times, in 1477/8, 1482/3 and 1502/3. He was very wealthy and owned land and property in, for example, Gayton, Gayton Thorpe, West Lynn and Dersingham as well as in Lynn and Gaywood. In his will, dated 3 May 1510, Thomas Thorseby left a very large number of bequests but one in particular is of great interest, his lands in Gaywood that are believed to comprise the bequest on which the Grammar School was founded.

> Item: I will that when Sir Thomas Grante, now being Charnel priest in Lenne, do leave the same service, and Sir Robert Burgh, priest, come into the same service and the same Sir Robert do teach and learn six children freely at grammar and song, sufficiently to maintain the choir in St. Margaret's Church in Lenne, in divine service, then I will, immediately that same Robert Burgh shall enter into the said service, that my lands in Gaywode, besides Goldsmith's garden, late Wynton's, which I bought of the executors of one Ade, shall remain in feoffees' hands to the use of the said Sir Robert and of his successors after that, being priests of the said Charnel, upon condition that he or they after that shall be chosen into the said service, be an honest and learned priest in song and grammar, and that he or they do daily teach 6 children in grammar and song, sufficiently to maintain the said service in the said church as aforesaid, and so to endure for ever. And for default of any of the said priests made in teaching of the said six children freely, as is above written, contrary to this my last will, then I will that my right heir or heirs, at that time being, shall enter into the said lands, to have them and to their heirs this gift notwithstanding.
>
> Item: I will that the said charnel priest, and also the two priests that shall sing continually for my soul, shall have their convenient chambers in the college, newly by me builded in Lenne, to be assigned unto them by the master of the said college for the time being.... [1]

We know that Sir* Thomas Grant was still Charnel Priest in 1510:

> This day Sir Thomas Grant has accounted for three years' profit and the reparations of the Charnel. (22 March 1510) [2]

It seems unlikely that Robert Burgh became Charnel priest in 1510 since the Hall Book makes no mention of his appointment, but if he did, he was succeeded by Thomas Rix in 1511, Thomas Pokering in 1513 and John Thorpe in 1524:

> This day it is agreed by all the congregation that Master Thomas Ryxe shall have the Charnel within the churchyard of St Margaret's in Lynn for the term of life of the said Master Ryxe provided always that if the said Master Ryx be otherwise spiritually promoted that then he shall leave the Charnel. (18 June 1511) [3]
>
> This day it is agreed that Sir Thomas Pokeryng shall have the Charnel from Christmas forth as it shall be made unto him by the advice of the Council of the town. (18 November 1513) [4]
>
> And it is recorded on that same day a certain indenture under the Common Seal was delivered to John Thorpe, Master of the Charnel, by which the same John Thorpe was admitted as Master for

---

* As well as to knights and baronets the title 'Sir' was, up to the Reformation, given to priests who were not university graduates.

the term of his life in accordance with the same indenture.
(19 September 1524) [5]

It is not known whether in this period the income from the four pastures in Gaywood mentioned in Thomas Thoresby's will was claimed or whether the conditions of Thomas Thoresby's will were kept. However in 1534, when the Lynn Corporation chose William Leyton as Charnel Priest, it was stated that he was 'to perform the testament of old Mr Thoresby and maintain a grammar school.' (Figure 1.) This gives us the clear reference back to the will of 1510:

> This day the Mayor, Aldermen and Common Council have elect[ed] and chosen unto their Charnel Priest, William Leyton, chaplain, he to have it from Our Lady's Day next coming during his life natural except causes reasonable and he to perform the testament of old Mr Thoresby and maintain a grammar school and further to keep his houses and tenements in sufficient reparations according in all things as near as he can according as it has been used. (13 March 1534) [6]

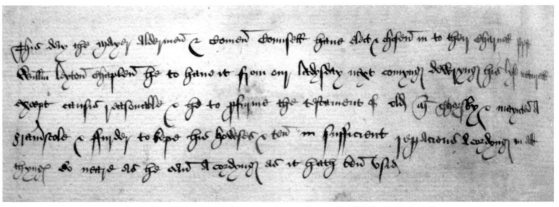

Figure 1 The first mention of a Grammar School in the Hall Books (13 March 1534)

The importance of teaching as an integral part of the work of the Charnel Priest is clear from the next two relevant entries in the Hall books. In July of 1538 Sir Richard Hall was appointed 'till Michaelmas next….to teach children in song and grammar frank and free.' Similarly from the beginning of October of that year when Thomas Person was chosen as the Charnel Priest he was 'to preach four times every quarter and freely teach six children.' 'Freely' in this context can be taken to mean free of charge:

> This day it is agreed that Sir Richard Hall shall keep the Charnel till Michaelmas next [to] come and he to have every month that he shall keep it 10 shillings and his service of the Trinity Guild and the same Sir Richard to teach children in song and grammar frank and free. (5 July 1538) [7]

> This day Thomas Person, priest, late friar, was chosen to be Charnel Priest, he to have for his salary eight pounds four shillings and licence to preach four times every quarter and freely to teach six children. (4 October 1538) [8]

What happened over the next few years is unclear. There are no further relevant entries in the Hall Book until 1548 and 1550. However sometime between 1538 and 1543 Thomas Thoresby's son, another Thomas, believing that the conditions in his father's will were not being kept, decided that he was entitled to take back the land in Gaywood left by his father to pay an income to the Charnel Priest. Nevertheless an agreement (Figure 2) was worked out in 1543 whereby the four pieces of pasture in Gaywood, referred to in Thomas Thoresby's will, would be granted to the Corporation, provided that it appointed a well-qualified priest who would teach six boys in grammar and song and these boys would pray daily for the soul of Thomas Thoresby and others:

Indenture, dated the first day of October, 35th of Henry VIII, between Thomas Thoresby of Mintlynn, Esquire, of the one part, and Richard Hunston, the Mayor, and Burgesses of the town of the other part, whereby after writing that Thomas, the father of the party, had by his will devised to the Mayor and Burgesses, four pieces of pasture in the parish of Gaywood, two of them in the occupation of Thomas Waters and two of John Yowle, upon condition that the Mayor and Burgesses should appoint a priest to be Master of the Charnel in King's Lynn, being born within the counties of Norfolk or Suffolk and of or above the degree of Master of Arts, who should instruct and teach six poor children in grammar and song, without reward and that the said children should nightly resort to the tomb of the said Thomas, the father, in the parish church of St Margaret and after evensong repeat certain psalms for the soul of the said Thomas and his ancestors and all good Christian souls with power of entry in case of default and after writing that Thomas, the son, had entered for the condition broken, the said Thomas, the son, nevertheless covenanted to confirm the land to the said Mayor and Burgesses, upon the conditions set forth in the next mentioned Indenture.

Indenture, dated 20th October, 35th Henry VIII, and the said Thomas Thoresby, the son, did thereby in pursuant of the covenant in the preceding deed, grant to the said Mayor and Burgesses and their successors, four pieces of pasture in the field of Gaywood, (without abuttals,) on condition that they should appoint a fit priest to celebrate mass in the Chapel called the Charnel Chapel in the

Figure 2 An indenture granting lands in Gaywood to the Corporation signed by Thomas Thoresby (the son), October 1543

Church of St Margaret, who should instruct six boys in grammar and plain song, without other reward; which boys should daily, on their knees, before the tomb therein mentioned, pray for the souls of the donor and other persons, repeating certain psalms; and it was provided that a failure of such appointment, or the performance of such services, the premises should revert to his son Thomas Thoresby and his heirs. [9]

Tracing the precise lands left by Thomas Thoresby has proved impossible. However there are a number of indicators. The Chamberlains' Accounts for 1553 list John Yowle as having two pastures near Goldsmith's Garden, Robert Maddy having one near Salter's Way and Thomas Waters having one near Salter's Way. [10] It is quite feasible that in the ten years since the Indenture between Thomas Thoresby and the Corporation one of the pieces had been given up by Thomas Waters.

Peter Sykes (2000) [11] has identified ten parcels of land owned by the Corporation in the area close to Goldsmith's Garden from the 1577 Records of Quit Rents. These are shown in Figure 3. The entry related to the area labelled 98 was quoted in the Introduction and a transcription is reproduced below:

> Item. The same held there in two pieces lying together, containing by estimation five acres of pasture, late in the occupation of Mr Watters, now in the occupation of [blank], lying in the same field, in breadth between the land of the Dean and Chapter aforesaid and the lands of the heirs of Edward Watters, sometime Trewys, and the lands of the said Robert Gervis. And the south head abuts upon the lands of the said Edward Watters, sometime Trewis, and the lands of the Dean and Chapter of Christ's Church, Norwich aforesaid.

This parcel of land had previously been let by the Corporation to a Mr Watters, almost certainly the same person as the Thomas Waters referred to in the 1543 Indenture above. The other three pieces of pasture are less easy to identify but those labelled 96 and 97 on the map are the two nearest to Salter's Way (Salter Road today) referred to in the Chamberlains' accounts mentioned above. The fourth piece of pasture could be any of the other seven numbered on the map. This may be as close as we can get to identifying the lands left by Thomas Thoresby in his will.

In the nineteenth century there was much debate about the origins of the Grammar School and whether it could be traced back to Thomas Thoresby's will. In his second of three reports to the Corporation on the history of the Grammar School, February 1836 [12], in which the details of the two indentures between Thomas Thoresby and the Corporation above are quoted, the Town Clerk, Frederick Lane, argues that 'it is unquestionable that by reason of the superstitious uses annexed to the grant, the land comprised in these deeds became vested in the Crown' by the Act of 4 November in the first year reign of Edward the Sixth, that is the Chantries Act of 1548. Under that Act property bequeathed by pious ancestors to promote the daily chanting of prayers for the dead could be confiscated.

Mr Lane cites a reference in Parkin (1762) [13] to an inquisition by certain commissioners in the third year of the reign of Queen Elizabeth (1561) preparatory to the Crown's taking possession of the forfeited land belonging to the Charnel House, and quotes the fact that the jury mentions a Charnel House in St Margaret's church yard which 'is now a school house'. Despite his assertion that the lands must have been forfeited to the Crown the Town Clerk admits that he could find no reference to such an inquisition or to the confiscation of Charnel lands in the Hall Books. As a result of further research he discovered a document dated 1577 [14] which he believed identified the land next to Goldsmith's Garden referred to in Thomas Thoresby's will and which

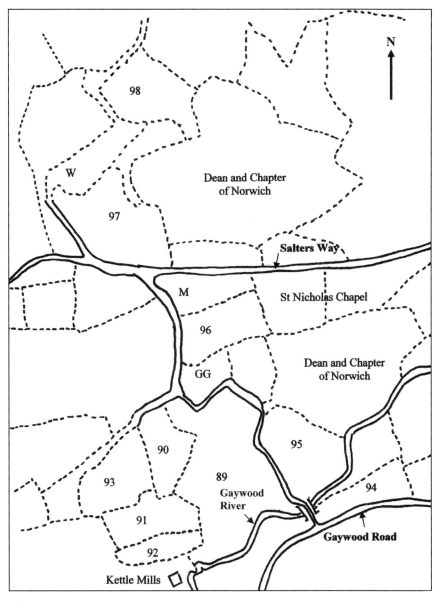

Key:

GG Goldsmith's Garden; W Edward Watters; M William Massen

Corporation Tenants:

89	Michael Revett	93	John Dynsdale	97	Robert Gervis
90	John Parmyter	94	Andrew Miller	98	(Mr Watters)
91	Richard Browne	95	John Grebby		
92	Richard Browne	96	John Grebby		

Figure 3 A sketch-map showing the possible location of the lands bequeathed by Thomas Thoresby to the Corporation in his will of 1510

was at that time owned by the Corporation. It seems most probable that this is the same document as that referred to by Peter Sykes and mentioned above. When the enclosure of the Parish of Gaywood took place in 1810 this land was still in the hands of the Corporation. However Mr Lane points out that there are no references in the Hall Books which recognise that these lands belonged to the Grammar School.

Another complicating factor when considering the endowments attached to the Charnel House is that it was endowed with lands before Thomas Thoresby's gift. In the second year of the reign of Richard III (1484) the Mayor and Burgesses granted to Thomas Gray, Bachelor of Divinity, the Charnel House and all the lands, meadows, feeding pastures and rents belonging to the said Charnel House on condition that prayers were said daily for the souls of Walter Cony, John Lock, Margaret, his wife, and others. [15] It is quite possible that such lands were confiscated to the Crown in 1548 or that it was those lands which were subject to the inquisition of 1561, if such took place.

The water is further muddied by a charter, dated 21 May in the second year of the reign of Edward VI (1549) which grants lands in Gaywood to the Corporation, the profits from which were to be used to build sea defences. These lands had come into the King's hands by force of the Chantries Act. Other lands were also granted that could be used for different purposes. [16] There is no specific mention of lands belonging to the Charnel. The Chantries Act did however include provision for the change of benefactions associated with superstitious purposes to be put to good uses such as the 'erecting of grammar schools to the education of youth in virtue and godliness'. It is possibly for this reason that some commentators such as William Richards, author of *The History of Lynn* (1812), in some private correspondence in 1818 [17], suggest that the land, having been seized by the Crown, was then granted to the Corporation, which felt obliged to apply the income to the original purpose.

From information supplied to it by the Town Clerk, the *Report of a Commission Enquiring into Public Charities*, (1834) [18], despite the Commissioners having seen the Indentures between Thomas Thoresby the son and the Lynn Corporation and despite the 1534 entry in the Hall Book referred to above which mentions Thomas Thoresby by name, nevertheless came to the conclusion that it had not 'met with any evidence tending to show that the lands now held by the Corporation in Gaywood were ever the property of Thomas Thoresby, or that the rents thereof were applied to the support of the school.' However, the Report accepts that from the time of Henry VIII the Corporation had kept up a grammar school as shown by the details in the Hall Books of the Masters and Ushers appointed. The first such mention comes in 1550 as we shall see in the next chapter.

2. The early years of the Grammar School

As we have seen in the first chapter of this book, in the first half of the sixteenth century the only references to education are those linked to the teaching of grammar and song by the Charnel Priest, but from 1550 we can trace the appointment of Schoolmasters by the Corporation right through to 1884 when the Lynn Grammar School became an endowed school with its own governing body.

The first such Schoolmaster was John Rackster, spelt in various ways in the Hall Book, but he was definitely not called Baxter as he is listed on the board in the King Edward VII School Hall, although as Figure 4 shows it is easy to see how the mistake was made. He held his post until 1570, albeit with a short break:

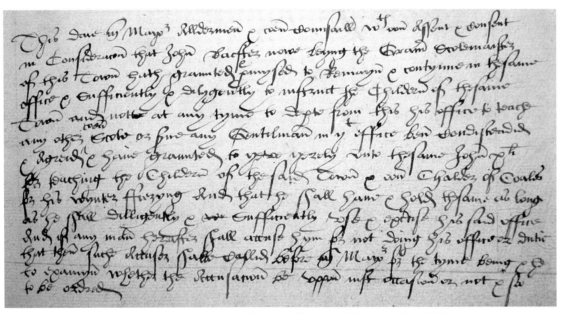

Figure 4 The first mention of a Schoolmaster in the Hall Books (16 November 1550)

> This day the Mayor, Aldermen and Common Council with one assent and consent in consideration that John Racster now being the Grammar Schoolmaster of this town has granted and promised to remain and continue in the same office and sufficiently and diligently to instruct the children of the same town and not at any time to depart from this his office to teach any other common school or serve any gentleman in that office [have] condescended and agreed and have granted to give yearly unto the same John ten pounds for teaching the children of the said town and one chalder* of coals for his winter firing and that he shall have and hold the same as long as he shall diligently and sufficiently use and exercise his said office. And if any man hereafter shall accuse him for not doing his office or duty that then such accuser shall be called before the Mayor for the time being and he to examine whether the accusation be upon just occasion or not and so to be ordered. (16 November 1550) [1]

The wording of the above might suggest that John Rackster was already the Schoolmaster in

---

* A chalder or chaldron was about one and a third of a ton.

1550 and he was simply being confirmed in his post. In a statement made by the then Head Master, the Reverend Thomas White, to the Schools' Inquiry Commission in 1865, it was claimed that the Master was re-appointed in 1550 on new conditions. There seems little evidence to support this assertion, although Dr White cites the sale of the 'old school house' in 1548 as demonstrating a break with the past:

> This day the Mayor, Aldermen and Common Council have bargained and sold unto Mr Baker the old school house with the garden thereunto adjoining for the sum of four pounds. (17 September 1548) [2]

We know that the Charnel Chapel, above the ossuary in which the bones taken from St Margaret's Churchyard were stored, was used as the school up to 1779. However it would seem that before 1548 the children were taught in one of the houses that formed part of the Charnel properties.

In the twenty years that John Rackster was the Master of the Grammar School several entries in the Hall Books refer to his salary and other payments. In 1551 he was granted the income from two tenements and two years later his salary was increased by 10 shillings per year:

> The Mayor, Aldermen and Common Council have granted to John Rakster the Schoolmaster two tenements wherein John Gibson and Richard Russer dwell so long as he shall be schoolmaster, paying yearly 20s. (30 July 1551) [3]

> This day it is condescended and agreed by the Mayor, Aldermen and Common Council that the Schoolmaster now being John Rackster shall have his fee of £10 10s. to him granted under the Common Seal for [the] term of his life doing his diligence in teaching children as he ought to do with a proviso that he shall not depart at any time from the service without the assent of the Mayor and Burgesses of this town. (18 November 1553) [4]

The next entry, in 1555, indicates that there has been a gap in his service but there is no indication of for how long or who took over in his place:

> The Mayor, Aldermen and Common Council have agreed and been contented to receive John Rakster, late Schoolmaster of this town, into the same office again and to have such wages as he had for the keeping of the same school in manner as he did. (30 September 1555) [5]

The following year, in addition to his salary, he was granted a house rent free as an additional perquisite:

> The Mayor, Aldermen and Common Council with one assent have agreed that John Rackster now Schoolmaster shall have his fee to him granted under the Common Seal accordingly as it was granted in Mr Palmer's year* and to have his house rent free. (28 April 1556) [6]

One of the most important developments early in the life of the school is the decision to allow the Schoolmaster to have another master, known as the Usher, as an assistant. Initially he was to be paid by imposing a levy on the parents of the pupils at the school. In 1561 this was set at 6 pence per quarter and seven years later was doubled:

> Memorandum that it is condescended and agreed that Robert Downes shall be Usher of the Grammar School and that he shall have towards his stipend of the parent of every child of the town that shall learn there 6 pence every quarter and of them of the country in like manner. (26 September 1561) [7]

> The Mayor, Aldermen and Common Council have this day condescended and agreed that John

---

*Mr Palmer was the previous mayor.

Rackster of this town and such other as succeed him in the same office shall and may have for his help and to the furtherance of the children which he shall teach such an Usher as they shall well like of for the time being, and for this time that Edward Graunte shall be the Usher, and that there may be taken and levied of the parents of every such child as shall be in the said school to learn grammar 12 pence quarterly towards the help of his living. (9 August 1568) [8]

Imposing a levy of this nature was certainly against the spirit of Thomas Thoresby's will. Whether or nor that was a relevant factor is unclear but the charge was removed in June of 1570 and replaced by a payment from the Corporation. At the same meeting of the Hall Mr Rackster was given an increase in his salary because of the esteem in which he was held:

Mr Mayor, Aldermen and Common Council have this day condescended and agreed that the order heretofore made touching the election of one Usher in the Grammar School and the stipend to him appointed by the town and by the parents of the children of this town shall be utterly void, frustrate and of none effect from Midsummer next coming.

And Mr Mayor, Aldermen and Common Council have now condescended and agreed that such as shall be Usher in the said Grammar School elected by the Corporation shall have for his stipend yearly of the commons £6 13s 4d to be paid quarterly.

And moreover Mr Mayor, Aldermen and Common Council have condescended and agreed that the Grammar Schoolmaster of this town shall have his fee and wages augmented that is to some £3 6s 8d over and besides that he now has, upon consideration of his well doing at the will and pleasure of this company. (16 June 1570) [9]

It is not known why Mr Rackster left his post so soon after his salary was increased but in October 1570 Mr Ralphe Johnson was invited to replace him and one year later he too had left and John Iverye became Schoolmaster:

At this day Mr Ivery was elected by Mr Mayor, Aldermen and Common Council to be Schoolmaster of the common Grammar School within this town. (10 October 1571) [10]

There are no relevant entries in the Hall Books for some ten years, but in 1580 the Corporation made a loan to Mr Iverye of £4 to buy books 'necessary to be in the school for his scholars':

Also this day there is delivered and lent Mr Iverye, Grammar Schoolmaster, £4 this day to buy books for the Grammar School to be repaid to this House again. (25 January 1580) [11]

This loan was repaid before the end of the year. Obviously at this stage the burgesses were not prepared to pay for the books, however necessary. They did accept responsibility for the cost of repairs to the Schoolmaster's house:

Also where before this time Mr Iverye received £4 to buy books necessary to be in the school for his scholars, now at this day the said Mr Iverye has made accompt of books by him bought and also has repaid the said £4.

Also allowed to him £5 for reparations and other necessary charges by him bestowed about his house. (26 September 1580) [12]

Two years later there is a very puzzling entry in the Hall Book:

Also whereas Mr Mayor, Mr Overend, Mr Hendry and Mr Clarke have delivered in writing here this day in the Hall a certain rate and order for the education of 24 children within the new house built for that purpose, now it is condescended and agreed that trial shall be made at the town's charge of the said order to see what good success the same shall take for six months and so to proceed further if it shall be found convenient. (29 August 1582) [13]

Vanessa Parker (1971) [14] claims that this entry indicates that the Grammar School was provided with a new building in 1582. However the entry makes no reference to the Grammar School and as we are certain that it was housed in the former Charnel Chapel at this stage one can only assume that this was some other educational initiative which may have come to nothing. No other references have been found.

The Hall Books report the successive appointments of Masters and Ushers and also changes in salary and other benefits. The salary of the Usher, for example, was raised in 1587 and again in 1588:

> Also at this day it is condescended and agreed by Mr Mayor, the Alderman and Common Council that there shall be an Usher provided for the Grammar School and that he shall have for his stipend eight pounds a year. (15 December 1587) [15]

> Also Richard Emott, Bachelor of Arts, is this day entertained to be Usher of the Grammar School for the stipend of £10 a year and if either the town shall mislike of him or he shall mislike of his place then upon half a year's warning he is to depart. (27 June 1588) [16]

Appendix 1 gives information about the Masters of the Grammar School up to 1919 and Appendix 2 lists the Ushers up to the middle of the eighteenth century, after which the appointments seem to have been made by the Master without reference to the Corporation. The records of arrivals and departures are not however complete. The following entry refers to the departure of a John Gibson who was the Usher before Richard Emott. We know from the Chamberlains' Accounts that 'Master Gybsone' was the 'hypodidasculus' or Usher in 1571/72. However details of his arrival and the departure of his predecessor, Master Pollard, appointed in 1570, have not been found:

> Also at the earnest request of John Gibson, clerk, late Usher of the Grammar School here, in consideration that the town shall be discharged of him and his family out of this town, there is given to the said John Gibson £5, which is delivered to William Wullman to see the same bestowed upon him. (26 July 1588) [17]

The provision of books for the scholars of the Grammar School has already been mentioned above. Another reference appears in 1590 following the death of Mr Sanderson, the preacher at St Margaret's Church:

> At this day Mistress Sanderson has delivered to the Hall here two books of Tully's works in Latin which were given by Mr Sanderson, her late husband, to remain for the school house of this town. (8 May 1590) [18]

At the end of 1590 John Iverye died and the Corporation chose as his successor Alexander Roberts who was also to replace Mr Sanderson:

> At this day Mr Mayor, the Alderman and Common Council have elected and chosen Mr Alexander Roberts, Master of Arts, to be Schoolmaster of the Grammar School of this town, to enter at the 2nd day of February next coming and to have for his stipend the same twenty marks [£13 6s 8d] a year and his dwelling over and besides in the house where Mr Iverye, late Schoolmaster, deceased, did dwell as he had the same.

> Also the said Mr Mayor, the Alderman and Common Council have elected and chosen the same Mr Roberts in lieu and place of Mr Sanderson, late preacher, deceased, to be the King's Lecturer, to read a lecture once every week, in consideration whereof he is to have forty marks a year to be paid to him by the town either of them quarterly by even portions. (18 January 1591) [19]

The responsibility for preaching once a week was obviously deemed more important than for running the Grammar School since the salary of the Schoolmaster was half that of the King's Lecturer. Also the salary of twenty marks stated above for the post of Schoolmaster is somewhat puzzling as John Rackster's salary was increased from ten pounds to ten pounds and ten shillings in 1553 and he was awarded a further £3 6s 8d in 1570, making £13 16 8d in all. Somewhere ten shillings would seem to have been lost.

Mr Roberts was appointed Rector of West Lynn in 1593, a post he was to hold until 1620, and so after only three years as Schoolmaster he was replaced by Nicholas Eston:

> At this day Mr Mayor, the Aldermen and Common Council have elected and chosen Nicholas Eston, Master of Arts, of Pembroke Hall in Cambridge, to be Schoolmaster of the Grammar School of this town in place of Mr Roberts, Bachelor of Divinity, late Schoolmaster there, during the good will and pleasure of the said Mayor, Aldermen and Common Council, and it is agreed that he shall have the like wages of twenty marks a year, to be paid by the town quarterly by even portions, as Mr Roberts before had, for the teaching of the burgesses' children and other poor men's children of this town and that he shall have the house in St James End by the mills, late in occupation of John Wrench, for his dwelling.

> Also the same day John Man, Bachelor of Arts, of Bennett College* in Cambridge is elected and chosen to be Usher of the said Grammar School during the like good will of the said Mayor and Burgesses, and he to have for his wages ten pounds a year, to be paid by the town quarterly by even portions, as his predecessor before had. (18 March 1594) [20]

The exact location of the schoolmaster's house at this time is unknown. St James End was an area to the east of what is today called St James Road and there was a corn mill in that area on the Millfleet, so the house must have been somewhere in that vicinity. A map showing the possible location (Figure 9) is included in Chapter 4. After about a year Nicholas Eston decided he did not want to live in the house in St James End and received instead an allowance of £3 per year:

> Whereas the Mayor, the Aldermen and Common Council have heretofore granted a tenement, wherein one John Wrench did lately dwell in St James End, unto Mr Eston, the Grammar Schoolmaster, in regard of his schoolmastership, now at this day, at the earnest suit of the same Mr Eston, the same Mr Mayor, Aldermen and Common Council are contented to take into their hands the said tenement, and to allow the said Mr Eston yearly in regards thereof three pounds, and, if the same shall be let for any greater rent, then the said Schoolmaster is to have the same, so long as he shall be Schoolmaster here. (26 September 1595) [21]

John Man, the Usher, was promoted to be Schoolmaster in 1597 in the place of Nicholas Eston and he remained in post until 1609. In 1600 the Corporation, with the consent of Mr Alexander Roberts, the former Schoolmaster, agreed that Mr Man should have the house in St James End by the town mills. Mr Roberts was to receive four pounds in lieu of the use of the house and grounds. However if he decided he wanted the house back then Mr Man was to be paid the four pounds instead.

When Mr Man took over as Master of the Grammar School Henry Royston (or Rosthorn) was appointed as the Usher. The conditions of service were much better than one might have expected. When he became ill in 1602 he was given leave of absence on full pay:

---

*Corpus Christi College.

Also whereas Mr Royston, Usher of the Grammar School, has of long time been visited with sickness and is desirous to be from his charge to lie in the country for a time between this and Midsummer next to see if by God's providence he can recover his health and to that end he has this day been a suitor to this House.

And Mr Man, Schoolmaster of the said school, of his own good will has promised in the meantime so much as in him is (respecting his own charges) to do his endeavour to supply the want of the said Usher, it is therefore ordered and agreed by Mr Mayor, the Aldermen and Common Council that the said Usher shall have liberty to be absent from the said charge for the time aforesaid. And yet nevertheless that he shall be allowed his stipend for so long of the said time as he shall be so absent for the cause aforesaid. (9 April 1602) [22]

The following year Mr Man was to receive the benefit of running water to his house, partly at his own expense but two thirds of the costs were to be born by the Corporation:

Also the same day at the humble petition of Mr Man, Schoolmaster of the Grammar School, now inhabiting a certain messuage or tenement belonging to the town situate and lying in a street called Saint James End, it is agreed by Mr Mayor, the Aldermen and Common Council that the same Mr Man shall have liberty to set a small pipe of lead without the corner against Baxters Row to the pipe of Mr John Spence, which conveys water to the pool of his brewhouse in Coldhirne (St), for the bringing of water from the same through the said small pipe to the said messuage or tenement so far forth as the setting of the same, given there be no stop or hindrance to the well serving of the said brewhouse with water, otherwise so that the same shall be set on in some other place to some other pipe where the same may best be taken of that water that comes from Middleton to service the conduit commonly called the New Conduit. The same to continue and endure during the good will and pleasure of the said Mr Mayor, the Aldermen and Common Council whereunto the said John Spence in form aforesaid has also consented and agreed. And it is agreed that the Town shall bear two thirds part of the charge of the said small pipe from the said pipe of the said Mr Spence. (15 August 1603) [23]

Note: Baxter's Row and Coldhirne Street are today called respectively Tower Street and Bridge Street.

In 1606 we have the first mention of governance in relation to the Grammar School. It was decided that two governors would be appointed to oversee the management of the school and later in the year various rules were agreed:

Also the same day it is agreed that there shall be two governors chosen by this house yearly on St John's Day to enter at Michaelmas following to see the ordering of the Grammar School and such orders put in execution as shall be thought good by the same House. (17 March 1606) [24]

Item. At the same time divers good orders were proposed for the government of the common free Grammar School in the said town of King's Lynn. And it is now ordered by the consent of the Mayor, the Aldermen and Common Council that the said orders shall from henceforth be duly observed, kept and performed and that the said orders shall at their charge be written in two fair tables and one of the same tables shall be hung openly in the said school and the other in the Council House of the said town. And that Mr Mayor, that is now Mr Matthew Clarke, and Mr Robert Gawsell, the Town Clerk, are made governors of the said school from Michaelmas to the Feast of St. Margaret then next following, for one school year. (19 September 1606) [25]

A set of rules for the ordering of the Grammar School is preserved in the Borough Archives but these bear the date 1662 [26] when they were 'again confirmed' by the Bishop of Norwich. It is possible that these may have replaced those agreed in 1606 but more likely they are the same. The rules are re-produced by Henry Harrod (1874) [27], who suggests that they probably date from a hundred years before 1662. He says that they were not peculiar to Lynn and were similar to those in use in many other grammar schools.

There are thirty-two rules in all, divided into sections concerned with Piety, Letters (the curriculum), Manners and Order. Pupils today would be aghast at being told they had to say prayers at half-past six in the morning and at five in the evening and that they would learn about the Faith on Saturday afternoons; neither would the school hours, from six in the morning to five in the afternoon, be welcome, even with a two-hour break for dinner from 11 o'clock to 1 o'clock. Good behaviour was obviously very important. Anyone 'who either in church or in public does not conduct himself modestly' would be punished as would 'brawling, fighting, noise, pilfering, obscenity and oaths.' Although school uniform was a thing of the future, there was a rule which said: 'Let no one come to the school with uncombed head, face and hands unwashed, dirty shoes and torn hose, or slovenly dress.' The old adage, cleanliness is next to godliness, obviously applied. There was even good advice for the masters, who had to 'arrange the course of study neither all at once nor confusedly, but leisurely, illustrating extensively with examples. Let them never go on to new lessons unless the former are known and fully understood.'

The Lennensian, the magazine of King Edward VII School, (December 1930), in which the rules are reprinted, also carried some delightful cartoons illustrating three of them: Rule 16, which insists on respect for one's betters (Figure 5); Rule 28, which allows for the exclusion of those who were unsuitable either by aptitude or laziness (Figure 6); and Rule 32 on the need for exercise

Figure 5 Rule 16.
In the streets, where magistrates, men of years or notability may be, let the head be uncovered and the way given to them, and let the Master reprove those who neglect to do so.

(Figure 7).   The Editor pointed out that the educational ideals of those days differed in many ways from their own and that a comparison of existing rules and methods with those from that time furnished food for thought. That certainly holds good today. The full rules are reprinted in Appendix 3.

Figure 6 Rule 28. Let the loiterer, the dull, the idle, the blockhead, and those who are slow in capacity and too little apt for learning, after three years, when the Master has with certainty ascertained their capacity and disposition, be sent by the Governors from the school to other business for which they are fit.

When Henry Allston was appointed Schoolmaster as from 25 March 1609 it was decided that Mr Man should be allowed to stay in the house in St James End until midsummer:

> Also it was agreed that Henry Allston shall be Schoolmaster of the Grammar School of this town, in the place of Mr Man, to begin his entrance at the Feast of the Annunciation of our Lady next and to have the fee and dwelling in the house appointed for the Schoolmaster as has been used, provided that the said Mr Man shall hold the said house until Midsummer next, and provided further that the said Mr Allston shall hold the said place of Schoolmaster only during the good will and pleasure of the Mayor, Aldermen and Common Council. (31 October 1608) [28]

In the event Mr Roberts must have decided that he would like to have the house again as he was promised he could in 1603:

> And it was agreed that Mr Allston, Schoolmaster, shall have £4 a year allowed unto him by the Mayor and Burgesses to be paid quarterly in respect that the school house is enjoyed by Mr Alexander Roberts. (14 July 1609) [29]

In the sixteenth and seventeen centuries there were various mentions in the Hall Books of outbreaks of the plague in Lynn. One of them, in 1610, makes specific mention of the need, as a precaution, to close the Grammar School:

And whereas it hath pleased God to visit this town at this time with the infection of the plague, therefore for the prevention of such danger as may further happen (if in case the same increase), it is agreed that the Master of the Grammar School shall have liberty at his will this week to break up the said school and to discontinue the same during the good will and pleasure of the Mayor and Aldermen of the Borough or the greatest part of them. (23 July 1610) [30]

On a number of occasions over the years the performance of the Master of the Grammar School disappointed the members of the Corporation. Mr Allston was dismissed in 1612 although no reason is given:

Also Mr Mayor, the Aldermen and Common Council have removed Henry Alston from being Schoolmaster of the Grammar School of this town and have agreed that during the time that he continues, until another Schoolmaster may be provided, he shall have his ordinary wage and at his departure shall be bestowed upon him twenty marks [£13 6s 8d] more. (25 August 1612) [31]

When a new Master, a Mr Armitage, Christian name unknown, was appointed later in 1612 the salary was considerably increased, possibly because they felt the need to attract a better quality of person for the post:

At this day it was agreed by Mr Mayor, the Aldermen and Common Council that from henceforth the yearly fee and stipend of the Schoolmaster of the Grammar School shall be 40 marks [£26 13s 4d] and he shall further have the use or benefit of the house in St. James End which usually heretofore has been appointed to the Schoolmaster without anything paying therefore but, for that the said house is granted to Mr Roberts, it is meet that the said Schoolmaster shall have allowed unto him, until the term of his years be expired, £4 per annum as the last Schoolmaster had. (2 October 1612) [32]

Figure 7 Rule 32. Forasmuch as the powers as well as of our minds as of our bodies are not only limited but also weak, for relief thereof let the Master give the scholars permission every Thursday afternoon, after two, for play and exercise, nevertheless upon condition that the games are of a sort which have innocence combined with enjoyment.

Also it is agreed that Mr Armitage of Emmanuel College shall be sent for to be the Schoolmaster of the Grammar School in this town if he will accept the same. (9 October 1612) [33]

Although the above shows that Mr Roberts, the Schoolmaster before Nicholas Eston, was still living in the house in St James End, the following year when his twenty-year lease ran out it was given to Mr Armitage:

Also it is agreed that from henceforth Mr Roberts, one of the preachers of God's word within this borough, shall be yearly allowed, for increase of his fee, four pounds in consideration that his grant made heretofore of the Grammar School house is expired at St Michael last and that now Mr Armitage is to enjoy the same. (8 October 1613) [34]

Soon after the appointment of Mr Armitage, it was decided that the Usher would receive an increase in salary to cover the cost of his food and lodging. In recent years the Usher had been paid £10 per year and his board had been provided by the Mayor:

Also it was agreed that an Usher shall be chosen for the Grammar School and that he shall have for his fee and to board him £16 per year. (18 December 1612) [35]

One of the longest serving Ushers, Mr Edward Laborne was appointed in 1613 and died in office in 1642. There are several entries which refer to him in the Hall Books, including one indicating that he acted as Master after the death of Mr Robert Robinson, Schoolmaster 1619 to 1625. The second entry refers to a payment of £4 to the Usher from the money paid by boarders. This would be in addition to his normal salary:

At this day, upon the petition of Mr Edward Laborne, Usher of this Grammar School, Mr Mayor, the Aldermen and Common Council have bestowed upon him towards the charges of his commencing Master of Arts this present year the sum of five marks. (20 June 1617) [36]

Also Mr Mayor, the Aldermen and Common Council have nominated and chosen Mr Robinson to be Schoolmaster of the Grammar School of this town in the place of Mr Armitage, lately deceased. And that Mr Laborne, now Usher of the said school, shall have allowed unto him yearly £4 out of the country scholars' payment which shall be under his tuition and the same to be paid unto him quarterly by the Master of the school. (18 January 1619) [37]

Also it is granted that Mr Laborne, Usher of the Grammar School, shall have twenty nobles [10 marks or £6 13s 4d] paid unto him for his pains taken since the decease of Mr Robinson, late Schoolmaster of the said school. (27 November 1626) [38]

These entries show that two of the Grammar School Masters died while still in the post, Mr Armitage in 1618 and Mr Robinson in 1625. The strong link between the Grammar School and Emmanuel College, Cambridge will be considered in the next chapter but it is interesting to note that when Mr Armitage died the Corporation wrote to the Master of Emmanuel to ask him to help them find a replacement:

At this day is agreed that a letter shall be written by Mr Mayor and the Aldermen to Cambridge to Master Doctor Chadderton to entreat him to procure a Schoolmaster for the Grammar School of this town in the stead and place of Mr Armitage, Schoolmaster, lately deceased. (20 November 1618) [39]

The benevolence of the Corporation at this time is demonstrated by its attitude towards Mr Robinson's wife after his death. She was to receive financial support for many years, the first time in 1626 when she was given her late husband's salary for the period from Michaelmas to Christmas, even though he had died in the middle of November. There are also numerous Hall Book entries up to 1652 in which she was granted various sums from thirty shillings to three pounds:

> At this day it was granted by Mr Mayor, the Aldermen and Common Council that Mistress Robinson, the widow of Mr Robinson, late Schoolmaster of this town, deceased, shall have the sum of £6 13s 4d paid unto her by the Chamberlains of this town for the quarter of the year wherein he died ended at Xmas last, notwithstanding that he departed this life before Xmas, about the middle of November. (27 February 1626) [40]

> It is this day ordered that Mistress Anne Robinson, the widow of Mr Robinson, the late Schoolmaster in this town, shall have delivered unto her the sum of 40s out of the poor box in this House, as the courtesy of this House in regard of her poverty and great necessity, which is delivered to Mr Mayor to give her accordingly. (27 September 1652) [41]

When Ambrose Fishe was appointed Master of the Grammar School in 1626, Robert Woodmansea in 1627 and John Rawlinson in 1635 each was granted the usual salary and the dwelling house commonly enjoyed by the Schoolmaster. Whether this is the house in St James End previously occupied by Mr Roberts or another is unclear. In 1635 the Grammar School is referred to, for the first time, as the Free School and this is commonly the case until the 1730s:

> At this day Mr John Rawlinson, Master of Arts, of St John's College in Cambridge, was by this House with general consent elected to be Chief Master of the Free School within this borough, in room and place of Mr Woodmansea of late gone out of the said place, to hold the said place upon the same fee and terms in all respects as the said Mr Woodmansea held the same, during the good will and pleasure of the Mayor and Burgesses.

> Also at this day the House, upon the departure of Mr Woodmansea, is pleased to bestow upon him £6 in regards of some cost he has bestowed about his dwelling house, to be paid by the Chamberlains; he leaving behind him the sink of stone with the dresser and shelves and other things fastened to the house. (23 March 1635) [42]

The responsibility of the Schoolmaster for the purchase of books was highlighted above but by the late 1620s the Corporation clearly saw it as part of its responsibility:

> At this day Mr Mayor brought into the Hall a new dictionary, well bound, called *Minshew his Dictionary* containing nine several languages, and the same cost thirty shillings which is disbursed by Mr Mayor, and it is delivered to Mr Woodmansea, Schoolmaster of this Grammar School, to be carefully kept in the school for the benefit of the scholars there from time to time. (23 November 1627) [43]

> At this day it is ordered by the House that certain books hereafter named propounded by Mr Rawlinson, Schoolmaster, to be very useful and necessary to be bought and to remain in the school house of this borough for the use of the scholars there from time to time shall be accordingly bought and provided by the Chamberlains at the town charge and committed to the charge and custody of Mr Rawlinson and his successors videlicet: Cooperi [Thomas Cooper's]Thesaurus Romano Britannicus, Rideri [John Rider's] Dictionarium Anglo-Latinum, Scapulae [Joann Scapula's] Lexicon Graeco-Latinum, Garthii Lexicon Latino-Graecum, Erasmi [Erasmus's] Adagia, Decinius de Graecis Epithetis, Colman de Graecarum Sillabarum Quantitate, Smetius de Latinarum Silllabarum Quantitate. (10 April 1635) [44]

As mentioned above, from about 1548 the school was located in a room in what had been the Charnel Chapel in St Margaret's Churchyard. Over the years it inevitably needed repairs and improvements as did the Schoolmaster's house. The earliest details found of repairs being carried out is shown in Figure 8, an extract from the Chamberlains' Accounts (with a transcription.) [45] This lists some repairs to the school in 1600 and gives an interesting insight into the costs of labour and materials at that time. The daily rate for a skilled workman seems to have been about one shilling a day. Assuming a six day week, that could give an annual income of up to £15 per year. The Schoolmaster's salary in 1600 of £13 6s 8d and a house worth £4 per year was therefore not very generous. However as we have seen the salary was doubled in 1612.

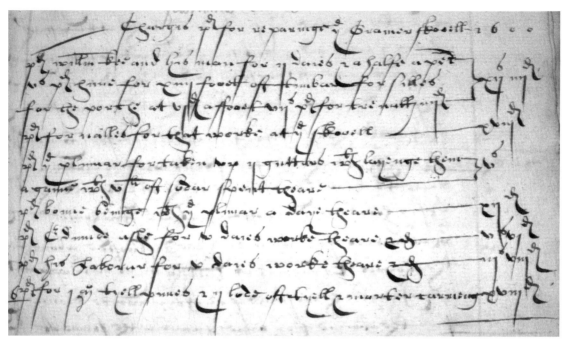

Charges paid for repairing the Grammar School 1600

Paid William Kee and his man for two days and a half a piece - 5s. Paid him for 14 feet of timber for sills for the porch at 6d per foot - 7s. Paid for trenails – 4d. [Total] 12s 4d. Paid for nails for that work at the school - 18d. Paid the plumber for taking up two gutters with laying them again with 6 lbs of solder spent there – 5s. Paid Bonne being with the plumber a day there -12d. Paid Edmund Ash for 5 days work there – 5s 6d. Paid his labourer for 5 days work there – 3s 8d. Paid for one quarter of tile pins and 2 loads of tiles and mortar carrying – 18d.

Figure 8 An extract from the Chamberlains' Accounts for 1599-1600, with transcription

The prices of some goods in 1625 may help to put wages and salaries in the early seventeenth century into some perspective: a pound of beef – 7d; a chicken - 4d; a pound of butter – 3½d; a pint of best claret – 3d; a pound of cheese – 2½d; and a pint of beer – a halfpenny. You could buy a thousand bricks for 14 shillings and rent a room or a stable for 4d per week. [46]

But to return to the Grammar School, another example of work done to improve the school room was carried out in 1635 when a louvre was installed:

> At this day it is ordered that a louvre in the middle of the Free School shall be erected and made for the better making of a fire here in winter time. (14 September 1635) [47]

In the middle of the seventeenth century major work was done on the Schoolmaster's house as we shall see in Chapter 4, but before that I intend to trace the links between the Grammar School and some Cambridge Colleges.

3. Scholarships and Awards to Cambridge

The early seventeenth century saw the first link established with a college in the University of Cambridge and that was with Emmanuel. The college was founded in 1584 by Walter Mildmay, Chancellor of the Exchequer to Elizabeth the First, and it was the first wholly new college since the Reformation.

In his will dated 14 April 1585 John Titley expressed his intention to establish a 'scholarship or fellowship at the new college called Emmanuel College in Cambridge' and his wife, Elizabeth, in her will dated 14 February 1595, bequeathed the sum of £130 to the Mayor and Burgesses of King's Lynn to maintain two scholars at Emmanuel. It was expected that the money would produce a yearly income of £9 15s of which £8 would fund the two scholars, twenty shillings would be paid to the College and fifteen shillings to the Corporation. At a meeting of the Corporation on 19 December 1603 it was agreed that the fifteen shillings allocated to them, together with a further twenty-five shillings from the town revenues, should be added to the £8, making £10 in all, to support the two scholars. The awards would be referred to as *Lynn Scholarships or Mr Titley's Scholarships*:

> Whereas Mistress Titley, widow deceased, did appoint by her will one hundred and thirty pounds to be paid to the Mayor and Burgesses of this town to the intent that they should from time to time put out the same at eighteen pence in the pound for the year, amounting to nine pounds fifteen shillings, whereof eight pounds to fund two scholars in Emmanuel College in Cambridge for the year, if the Master and Fellows of the same college will agree thereto, twenty shillings to be to the use of the Master and Fellows and the other fifteen shillings to the use of the Mayor and Burgesses for their painstaking about the same. It is now agreed by the Mayor, the Aldermen and Common Council, for the better maintaining of the said two scholars in the said college, that the said eight pounds shall be augmented to ten pounds a year to make each scholarship five pounds a piece viz. the said fifteen shillings devised to the Mayor and Burgesses as aforesaid to be added thereto and twenty five shillings more out of the Town's revenues. And it is also agreed that the said one hundred and thirty pounds shall be called in by the town and the cause to be followed with effect for the sending forth of the said two scholars according to the meaning of the will. (19 December 1603) [1]

A copy of the agreement between the Mayor and Burgesses of King's Lynn and the Master and Fellows of Emmanuel College dated 27 October 1606 is referred to in Hall Book 6 and at the same meeting it was indicated that the first Titley Scholar would be John Dains (or Daynes):

> Also at this day Mr Mayor and the Aldermen and Common Council have sealed and delivered one part of the indenture of the covenant for the maintenance of two scholars according to the late will and testament of Mr Titley and Mistress Titley which was delivered into the hand of Thomas Oxburgh Esq.

> Also at this day John Dains was elected one of the scholars which should be maintained at Cambridge in Emmanuel College according to the wills of Mr Titley and Mistress Titley and the covenant between the Mayor and Burgesses of this borough and the Master and Fellows and Scholars of the said College. (27 October 1606) [2]

It did however take until the following February before all the formalities had been sorted out and the first two Titley scholars were formally nominated:

> At this day John Dains, the son of John Dains, and Thomas Robinson, the son of Thomas Robinson,

were elected out of the Grammar School of this borough as two of the most sufficient scholars of the said school and were commended unto the Master, Fellows and Scholars of Emmanuel College under the Common Seal of this borough, according to one deed indented made between the said Master, Fellows and Scholars and the Mayor and Burgesses of this borough, which deed bears the date the 27th day of October last.

At this day Robert Gawsell, Town Clerk, delivered into the House the counterpart belonging to this town made between the Mayor and Burgesses of this borough and the Master, Fellows and Scholars of the University of Cambridge for two scholars to be maintained according to Master Titley and Mistress Titley's wills. (10 February 1607) [3]

Throughout the seventeenth century scholars from the Grammar School were regularly nominated by the Corporation and the twice-yearly payments to Emmanuel College were recorded in the Hall Books, as shown in the examples below:

Also £5 10s of the interest of money of Mistress Titley was delivered to Mr Atkyn to be sent to Emmanuel College for the half year ended at the Feast of the Annunciation of Our Lady last for the maintenance of the two scholars kept there according to Mistress Titley's will. (7 April 1609) [4]

At this day William Atkyn brought into the Hall an acquittance, dated 30th October 1613, under the hand of Lawrence Chadderton, Doctor of Divinity, Master of Emmanuel College in Cambridge, testifying the receipt of £5 10s for a half year due at St Michael last past to the said college, which money is for the maintenance of two scholars there, according to the testament and last will of Mr Titley. And the said £5 10s was paid to the said William Atkyn. (3 December 1613) [5]

Hall Book entries such as the ones above can be read twice a year from 1607 to 1616. After that they are more irregular but the money must have been paid as scholars were continuously nominated by the Mayor and Burgesses in the seventeenth century, as can be seen by the list in Appendix 4.

One of the early scholars to be awarded a Titley Scholarship was Bartholomew Adrian who was at the university from 1611 to 1618:

Also at this day Mr Mayor, the Aldermen and Common Council have nominated and appointed Bartholomew Adrian, one of the scholars of the Grammar School of this town, to be scholar in Emmanuel College in Cambridge, according to the tenor of Mr Titley's will and to enjoy the benefit of a scholarship there in the stead and place of [John] Daynes, late scholar there who enjoyed that place there and is lately departed from thence. (18 February 1611) [6]

In addition to the benefits of the Titley Scholarship in terms of tuition and accommodation Master Adrian was also given additional financial support as shown by the following extract from the Hall Books:

Also whereas Bartholomew Adrian, one of the scholars of this Grammar School, was lately admitted into one of the scholarships of Emmanuel College, called Lynn Scholarships or Mr Titley's Scholarships, at this day it was agreed that the Mayor and Burgesses shall cause him to be furnished with such apparel, bedding, books and furniture as shall be needful at this present [time] to set him forthwith, not exceeding the sum of £10. (12 April 1611) [7]

In fact Bartholomew Adrian was to receive very generous support from the Corporation over the time he was at Cambridge: £3 6s 8d in 1612 for the purchase of books, five marks in 1615 'towards his commencing this year Bachelor of Arts', £5 in August 1613, forty shillings in February 1616, a further £5 in September and another £3 in October the same year. In September 1617 he was awarded £4 'towards his maintenance at Emmanuel College' and finally he received £6 in 1618:

….it was agreed upon the humble petition of Bartholomew Adrian, scholar of Emmanuel College in Cambridge, to bestow upon him towards his commencement of Master of Arts this year, £6, which is to be paid by the Chamberlains. (27 March 1618) [8]

As the above information suggests, the Titley Scholars were by no means all the sons of rich men. Thomas Walker (nominated in October 1623), whose father was a cook, and Richard More, the son of a joiner, were both given additional support:

Also five marks was taken out of the Hall and delivered to Mr Mayor towards the apparelling of Thomas Walker, son of William Walker, cook, who was chosen to one of Mr Titley's Scholarships to go out of the Grammar School to Emmanuel College in Cambridge. (8 December 1623) [9]

Also an instrument nominating the election of Richard More, late one of the Grammar Scholars of this School, to have and enjoy one of the scholarships in Emmanuel College in Cambridge, called Lynn Scholarships or Mr Titley's Scholarships, was sealed with the Common Seal of this borough. Also it is granted at the humble petition of Richard More, joiner, that 33s 4d shall be paid by the Chamberlains for the defraying of the charges in the university for his son, the above named Richard More, who is chosen scholar as above said. (14 July 1626) [10]

The first disagreement between the Corporation and Emmanuel College was in 1639 when Thomas Theoderick was nominated to a Titley Scholarship but was evidently deemed unsuitable for some reason, as the following extracts from the Hall books indicate:

This day it is ordered that the covenant between the Mayor and Burgesses of this borough and the Master and Fellows of Emmanuel College in Cambridge, concerning Mistress Titley's gift for a poor scholar's allowance and admittance there, shall be delivered unto Mr Leek, Town Clerk, to the end he shall thereupon frame a letter to the said Master and Fellows concerning one Thomas Theoderick, a poor scholar elected and sent thither by this House and contrary to the said covenant refused to be accepted of in the said college. (13 December 1639) [11]

This day it is ordered that Mr Mayor on behalf of this House shall write a letter to Emmanuel College in Cambridge in answer of a late letter of theirs to Mr Mayor concerning the declaration of the House's consent and desire to have Thomas Theoderick enjoy the privilege and benefit of one of the Lynn Scholarships of Mr Titley's gift as a poor scholar in the college. (7 March 1640) [12]

The outcome of this correspondence is unknown. However according to *Venn's Alumni Cantabrigienses* [13] Thomas Theoderick was admitted to Emmanuel on 23 February 1639 as a sizar or poor student. When he left is unclear. He does not seem to have been awarded a degree but was ordained in the diocese of Norwich in September 1644.

One grant which was specifically aimed at poor scholars was Peirson's Gift. In his will dated 22 October 1623 John Peirson, or Pierson as it is also spelt, a carpenter, left some property in Lathe Street (now Nelson Street) which was sold for £250 by the Mayor and Town Clerk and, after certain legacies had been paid, the residue, which came to £183 6s 8d, was to be used to provide three gifts each of 40 shillings per year, including one to fund a poor scholar of the Lynn Grammar School to go to any college in Cambridge:

And also one hundred fourscore three pounds six shillings and eight pence residue thereof to the intent that the said Mayor and Burgesses and their successors shall bestow forever in the name and remembrance of the said John Peirson upon some poor scholar from time to time yearly which shall go out of the Grammar School of this town and live in any college in Cambridge, forty shillings during the first seven years of his abiding there. And upon the poor people in the alms houses in this town yearly in the Lent season other forty shillings, and upon the poor people in Stonegate ward to be distributed by the discretion of the Mayor for the time being or the Alderman of the said ward yearly in the Lent season other forty shillings. (8 July 1625) [14]

Appendix 4 also lists those granted the Peirson Award. The first person to benefit was John Fawcett:

> Also it is ordered that John Fawcett, son of Richard Fawcett, tailor, late scholar in this Grammar School and now a scholar in Cambridge, shall be allowed 40s a year, during the good will and pleasure of the Mayor and Burgesses, for his maintenance in that university, according to the last will of John Peirson, deceased. (14 January 1625) [15]

As can be seen from the date of the entry above Master Fawcett was awarded forty shillings before the sale of the property in Lathe Street. In fact the eventual owner, Richard Jolles, was at this stage paying rent for it. It is not clear whether the following entry represents a part payment for the first year:

> Also the said Mr Mayor and Town Clerk have paid this day into the Hall which they received of the aforesaid Richard Jolles for the rent of the said messuage and premises until the same were sold, four pounds, which four pounds is delivered to Mr Mayor and it is ordered to be presently distributed as follows: videt 26s 8d parcel thereof to one John Fawcett, a scholar lately out of this school to Christ's College in Cambridge; 26s 8d one other parcel thereof to the poor in the almshouses in this town; and the other 26s 8d amongst the poor people in Stonegate ward. (8 July 1625) [16]

It was not unusual for the Peirson Gift to be awarded to Titley Scholars as an additional measure of support. Thomas Walker, mentioned above, was awarded the forty shillings in the years 1628, 1629 and 1630 and the following year he received additional support when he took his MA:

> Also it is granted that the Mayor and Burgesses shall bestow upon Thomas Walker, son of William Walker, cook, scholar in Emmanuel College in Cambridge, £5 towards the charges of his commencing Master of Arts this year, which money to be paid by the Chamberlains. (1 July 1631) [17]

Another gift left specifically for poor scholars was bequeathed by Alexander Hall. In his will, dated 27 July 1597, Mr Hall left a warehouse in Fincham Street (now New Conduit Street) on the corner of High Street, to his cousin, William Hall, on condition that he and his heirs would pay 40s per year, for up to seven years, to a poor scholar born in King's Lynn and going to the University of Cambridge. This was to continue 'ever after'. The money was to be paid within eighteen days of a valid request. If William Hall or his heirs defaulted on the gift then the warehouse was to be given to the Mayor and Burgesses with the same conditions attached. As with the Peirson Award no particular college was specified.

However it is not until more than fifty years after the will was proved that the first reference is found to an award being made. The recipient, Thomas Thurlin(g), who in the seventeenth century was to fund an exhibition himself, was also to have Peirson's Gift:

> It is also ordered that Thomas Thurling now a scholar at St John's College in Cambridge shall have the allowance of forty shillings per annum the gift of Mr Alexander Hall out of a warehouse in Fincham Street during the good will and pleasure of this House. And also that he shall have paid him forty shillings more yearly out of the gift of John Peirson that was formerly paid to Bennett Revely, this House being informed that the said Bennett Revely has left Emmanuel College. (18 September 1651) [18]

As the lists in Appendix 4 show these two awards were often made to the same person, since the value, even in the seventeenth century was relatively small.

In November 1654 Thomas Thurlin was awarded 20 nobles (£6 13s 4d) 'towards his charges in taking his degree' and three years later the Corporation was informed that he had been offered a fellowship at St John's College which would allow them to grant the Peirson and Hall Exhibitions to another scholar:

> It is this day ordered that in case Thomas Thurling (who is now as it is notified to this House preferred to a fellowship in Cambridge) shall accept of the same fellowship, then the allowance which is paid from this town to the said Mr Thurling be paid unto Edward Tilson, son of Edward Tilson, late of this town, anchor smith, who is ordered to be one of the scholars for this town in the room of the said Mr Thurling in case he accept of the said fellowship. (23 March 1657) [19]

More will be said of Thomas Thurlin below. Other names which are to appear again in future years are James Hayes and Richard Nesling. They were both pupils at the Lynn Grammar School who went on to Cambridge as Titley Scholars and later returned to the school as Ushers:

> It is this day ordered that James Hayes, the son of William Hayes of this borough, shall have one of the places or scholarships in Emmanuel College in Cambridge called Mr Titley's Scholarships lately enjoyed by Mr Michael Stukley with the salary or stipend to the same belonging and that a certificate of his election be made under the Common Seal of this borough. (22 February 1661) [20]

> It is this day ordered that Richard Nesling have one of Mr Titley's Scholarships in Emmanuel College in Cambridge lately enjoyed by John* Hayes the salary or stipend to the same belonging and that a certificate of his election be made under the Common Seal of this borough. (3 March 1665) [21]

A further award for scholars of the Lynn Grammar School became available in the seventeenth century but since this was paid directly to Trinity College there are no references to it in the Hall Books until the second half of the nineteenth century. It was known as Hopes's Exhibition. £3 8s 8d per year, for the maintenance of a poor scholar from the Free School in Lynn to go to Trinity College in Cambridge, was payable by the Rector of North Runcton near King's Lynn under an indenture, dated 19 January 1653, between Richard Hopes and the Master and Fellows of Trinity College, arising from the will of Thomas Hopes (03 March 1616). The money was to be paid to the College and the scholar was to be chosen by the Mayor of King's Lynn and the Master and Fellows of Trinity.

In contrast to the thirty or so Titley Scholars nominated by the Corporation in the seventeenth century, only six are listed in the eighteenth century. For a time the Corporation fell behind in its payments to Emmanuel College and as a result received a demand for the money from the College's solicitor. However, according to the first person to hold the scholarship since the turn of the century, Charles Phelps, nominated in 1731, no specific benefits had been received:

> Upon reading a letter from Mr Yorke, Attorney for the Master, Fellows and Scholars of Emmanuel College, Cambridge, directed to Mr Philip Case, setting forth that there is £88 due from the Mayor and Burgesses to that college for eight years arrears of an annuity of £11, the gift of Mr Titley, and adding that the society was come to a resolution to enforce a speedy payment of it. And upon reading an indenture, dated 27th October in the 4th year of the reign of King James the First [1606], between the Mayor and Burgesses of the one part and the Master, Fellows and Scholars of that College of the other part, by which the latter specifically covenanted with the former that the scholars (under the denomination of the Mr Titley's Scholars) sent from this Grammar School to that College shall have and enjoy freely the benefit and privileges of tuition and chambers and

---

*This kind of error is not uncommon in the Hall Books – the Christian name should be James. Elsewhere Hayes is written as Haes and Nesling as Neslyn.

studies, meet and convenient in that College. And upon the information now given to this House by the Reverend Mr Charles Phelps, late of the said Mr Titley's Scholars in that college, that he paid as much for his tuition and chambers there as any other scholars would have paid for the same. Now upon consideration had of the provisos, this House doth order that the Town Clerk write a letter in the name of this Corporation to the Master, Fellows and Scholars of that College signifying to them that as they have not performed their parts this Corporation think themselves by no means obliged to pay the arrears of money demanded of them. (20 October 1740) [22]

What the outcome of this correspondence was is unclear but Thomas Stona was nominated to a Titley Scholarship in 1744, as were John Fairfax Franklin in 1760, Henry Smith in 1771, William Hardyman in 1781 and Charles Lloyd in 1795. The award to Thomas Stona sets out more clearly than had been the case in the past what benefits the recipient of the Scholarship could expect to receive:

Ordered that Thomas Stona (son of the Revd. Mr Robert Stona, clerk,) educated at the Grammar School here and lately admitted a student in Emmanuel College, Cambridge, have Mr Titley's Exhibition money together with the arrears. And also that the said Thomas Stona have and enjoy freely the benefit and privileges of tuition and chambers and studies meet and convenient within the said college for seven years from his admission if he shall so long continue in the same college. (29 September 1744) [23]

Problems about the payment of the annuity to the college obviously continued because in 1756 and again in 1757 the Corporation would seem to have been in arrears:

Ordered that the arrears, due from the Corporation to the Master, Fellows and Scholars of Emmanuel College in Cambridge, be paid immediately by the Chamberlain. (5 November 1756) [24]

Ordered by the Mayor, Aldermen and Common Council that the Chamberlain do immediately after the receipt thereof pay the Master and Fellows of Emmanuel College in Cambridge the annuity and all arrears thereof due to them from this Corporation to Michaelmas last. (21 November 1757) [25]

A new award, this time for students to go to St John's College in Cambridge, was made available in the eighteenth century. The Reverend Thomas Thurlin, Doctor of Divinity, Rector of Gaywood from 1664 to 1714 and President of St. John's College, 1683 to 1714, left £200 in his will, dated 02 September 1708, to the Mayor and Burgesses of Lynn, on condition that they would pay £6 per year, for up to four years, for a poor scholar to go from the Grammar School to St John's College. This is the same Thomas Thurlin (also spelt Thurling and Thurlyn in some of the Hall Book entries) who had been a pupil at the Grammar School in Lynn and received help from the Corporation in the form of the Hall and Peirson Exhibitions from 1651 to 1657, in which year he was made a Fellow of St John's. Following his death in 1714 Thomas Thurlin was buried at St Faith's Church in Gaywood.

A draft agreement was drawn up by the Lynn Corporation in 1715 but it seems that the agreement was never ratified because a clause was added by the College which did not gain the approval of the Corporation. The College wanted to have the right to nominate a scholar from the Lynn Grammar School if none was proposed by the Mayor and Burgesses within six months of a vacancy occurring and, if no suitable candidate was forthcoming from Lynn, they wanted to be able to use the money to support a poor scholar from another Norfolk school. Nevertheless some six Thurlin Exhibitioners did go to St John's from the Lynn Grammar School in the eighteenth century as shown in Appendix 4. The first to be nominated was Henry Michelson in 1736:

Ordered that Doctor Thurlyn's Exhibition together with the arrears thereof be paid to Henry

Michelson, a poor scholar bred up in the Grammar School of this borough, towards his education in St John's College, Cambridge. (3 February 1736) [26]

The disagreement about who had the right to nominate Thurlin Exhibitioners re-emerged in 1774 and the original agreement was examined to check the facts:

Ordered that the Town Clerk do search for the will of Dr Thurlin or for the deed made between this Corporation and Saint John's College in Cambridge in relation to the Exhibition of the said Dr Thurlin to a scholar from the Lynn Grammar School to the said college, the said college pretending a right to nominate the scholar who shall be entitled to the said Exhibition which right of nomination this Corporation apprehend has always been in the Corporation. (28 November 1774) [27]

What does become clear by the second half of the eighteenth century and later is that the original intention of the donors that the Peirson, Hall and Thurlin awards should be for the benefit of poor scholars was not always followed. The sons of clergymen, who admittedly were not all rich, and even the sons of the Masters of the Grammar School were among the beneficiaries:

Agreed that Henry Lloyd, the son of Mr David Lloyd, Master of the Grammar School, now admitted of Trinity College in Cambridge, have the vacant Exhibitions of Hall and Peirson, of forty shillings each, and such arrears as are due for the same. (29 September 1781) [28]

Agreed and ordered that Peirson's Exhibition of forty shillings a year (now vacant) with the arrears thereof be paid to Stephen Allen the younger, (son of the Reverend Stephen Allen, Minister of the Parish of Saint Margaret within this borough), who has been educated at the Free Grammar School of this borough and is now admitted of one of the colleges in the University of Cambridge. (11 September 1793) [29]

Henry Lloyd was elected a Fellow of Trinity College in 1787 but he was only one of a number of scholars from the Lynn Grammar School to become College Fellows in Cambridge in the seventeenth and eighteenth centuries. As we have seen above, Thomas Thurlin was a distinguished Fellow of St John's College and, much later in the eighteenth century, Thomas Catton, a Thurlin Scholar, was to become a Fellow (1784 to 1838). He was a noted astronomer who was elected to a Fellowship of the Royal Society in 1821. Earlier that century two other former Thurlin Scholars, Henry Michelson and John Cott, had became Fellows of Clare and Corpus Christi Colleges in 1743 and 1752 respectively.

At Gonville and Caius College, Joshua Bassett and Robert Rolfe were elected Fellows in 1665 and 1744 respectively. In addition at least five former Titley Scholars became Fellows of Emmanuel College: Hampden Reeve in 1645; Michael Stukeley in 1660; William Needham in 1677; Gervaise Needham in 1685; and William Hardyman in 1788.

Another former Titley Scholar, Luke Eales, admitted to Emmanuel in 1649, became a distinguished physician. He was awarded the degrees of Bachelor of Medicine in 1654 and Doctor of Medicine in 1661 and became Physician to Charles ll. In 1670 he was granted the right to his own Coat of Arms.

More will be said on the various exhibitions to Cambridge in later chapters.

Having traced the origins of the links with Emmanuel, Trinity and St John's Colleges, it is now time to return to the history of the Grammar School in the seventeenth and early eighteenth centuries.

4. Mr Bell and Mr Horne

For nearly 100 years the Grammar School was under the Mastership of just two men, Edward Bell (1637 to 1678) and John Horn (1678 to 1730). Edward Bell had been a student at Magdalene College, Cambridge, gaining his BA in 1627/8 and his MA in 1631. He was the brother of Alderman Henry Bell who was the father of Henry Bell, the architect of the Customs House in Lynn.

> At this day the Mayor, Aldermen and Common Council have elected and chosen Mr Edward Bell, late of St Ives, Master of Arts, to be Master of the Free School of this borough, and to have the dwelling house and fees thereunto belonging as formerly, and in the room and stead of Mr Rawlinson, last Master there. (29 September 1637) [1]

Soon after his arrival, Mr Bell was invited to accompany the mayor on a visit to Norwich and was presented to the Chancellor of the Diocese. :

> Also Mr Mayor, accompanied by Mr Alderman Toll and Mr Bell, the Free School Master, are appointed to go to Norwich. Mr Mayor and Mr Toll to treat with the High Sheriff and others about the assessment for the ship of war for His Majesty's service and Mr Bell to be presented to the Chancellor as Free School Master. (6 November 1637) [2]

The discussion about taxes to be levied on the town for a warship came at a time when opposition to King Charles the First had already broken out in Scotland and within five years there would be Civil War in England. In that war King's Lynn was part of the Eastern Association on the side of the Parliamentarians not the King.

The Schoolmaster's house in Edward Bell's time was the one in St James Street, almost opposite the Greyfriars Tower, which in the nineteenth century was to become the site of the main Grammar School building. The last mention in the Hall Books of the house in St James End was in 1613 when it was transferred from Mr Alexander Roberts to Mr Armitage. Although the records do not show that a new house was found in the 24 or so years that followed before Mr Bell's appointment, it is difficult to see how his house which was directly opposite what is now the bingo hall could be described as near a mill.

Figure 9 shows an extract from W Rastrick's 1725 map of Lynn [3]. As mentioned above the Schoolmaster's house in the 1650s was in Fuller's Row (20), now St James Street, near to the corner with Baxter's Row (19), today called Tower Street. The original house assigned to the Schoolmaster in St James End must have been close to the Corn Mill (T). The map also shows the locations of All Saint's Church (B), the St James Workhouse (D), Greyfriars Tower (I), St Margaret's Church (A), the Guild Hall (L), the Grammar School (E) and the Oil Mill (S). The latter was not built until 1655 and so could not have been the mill referred to in descriptions of the location of the Schoolmaster's house from 1594 to 1613.

Repairs and improvements to the Schoolmaster's house and grounds are regularly reported in the Hall Books and the following three extracts show that by the seventeenth century responsibility for these was accepted by the Corporation:

> This day, upon the request of Mr Bell, the Schoolmaster, it is ordered that Mr Mayor, Mr Alderman Maye, Mr Alderman Bassett [and] Alderman Mr Nathaniel Maxie shall go to Mr Bell's house and view what walls and fencing is in their discretion fitting to be done for the enclosing of his garden or backside. And that the same shall be accordingly performed and done by the Chamberlain at

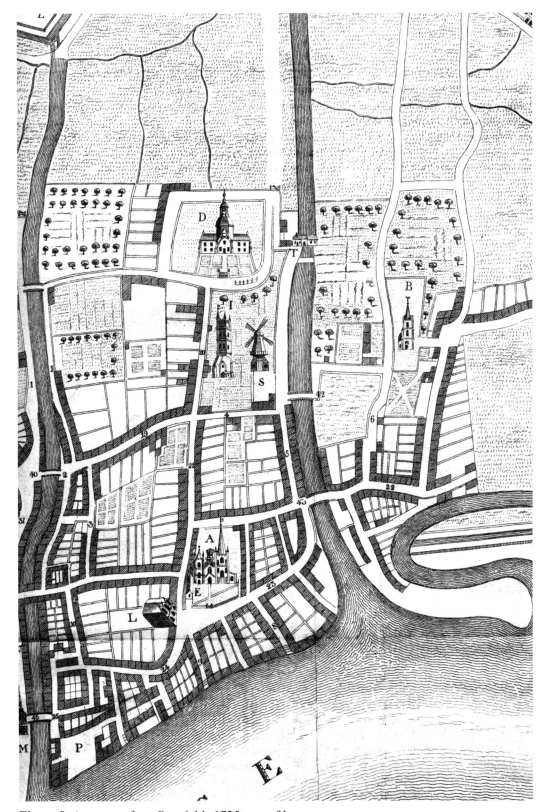

Figure 9 An extract from Rastrick's 1725 map of Lynn

the town charge. (22 February 1639) [4]

It is this day ordered that Mr Bartholomew Wormall, Alderman, Mr Jonas Scott, Alderman, Mr John Bassett, Alderman, and Mr Richard Browne, one of the Common Council, be desired to meet as a Committee or any three of them, whereof the said Mr Alderman Scott and the said Mr Richard Browne, the present Chamberlains to be two of the said Committee, to view the school house and to report to this House what charge it will be to this House to make a chamber over the hall of the said school house as it desired by Mr Edward Bell, the now Schoolmaster, in his letter presented to this House. (15 August 1653) [5]

It is this day ordered that Mr Bell, the now Schoolmaster, shall have allowed him eight pounds towards the making of a chamber on his hall with a chimney in it over the school house, and the Chamberlains are desired to pay the same to the said Mr Bell for that purpose. (22 August 1653) [6]

In 1659 major work on the Schoolmaster's house had to be carried out. Despite the fact that this re-building work took place during the mayoralty of his brother Henry, Edward Bell was required to pay one third of the cost. David Higgins (2005) [7] says this was because the school house was used for boarders as well as for day boys. Such boarders would provide extra income for the Schoolmaster. Extensive rebuilding was carried out and Higgins describes 'the restoration and enlargement of the schoolhouse in St James Street' as 'the most notable event' in Henry Bell's mayoralty – 'from a Bell point of view.'

Figure 10 The stone commemorating rebuilding work on the Schoolmaster's house in St James St. in 1659

Until 1752 the New Year in England began on Lady Day (25 March) not 1 January. The date of the following extract is before 25 March and hence 1658 in the old calendar. The building stone commemorating the building work (Figure 10) is therefore dated 1658/9:

It is this day upon the request of Mr Edward Bell, Master of the Free School within this borough, ordered that the forepart of his now dwelling house, being very much in decay, be forthwith put in good repair and the roof raised for his accommodation and that the manner of doing the same be left to the said Mr Edward Bell and the Chamberlains to do the same according to their discretion, the said Mr Edward Bell bearing one third part of all such charges whatsoever as shall be expended about doing the same. (23 February 1659) [8]

Both Edward Bell's son, Edmund, and his nephew Henry, who became the celebrated architect, were educated at the Grammar School. They went up to Gonville and Caius College in Cambridge in 1661 as Scholars. During this period, as we saw in the last chapter, there was a regular flow of students from the Grammar School to Cambridge, going as Titley Scholars to Emmanuel College or, some supported by the Peirson and Hall Exhibitions, to a number of other colleges.

Over the 41 years that Edward Bell was Master of the Grammar School he was assisted by a long series of Ushers. The first of these, Edward Laborne, first appointed in 1613, became ill and was dismissed in 1642 by the Corporation without much sign of gratitude for his long service. He died shortly after:

> This day by this House it is ordered that Mr Laborne, Usher of the Free School here, having been sick and still continuing so, whereby the school is much out of order for want of an Usher, shall be displaced from henceforth. And that Mr Bell, the Schoolmaster, shall be desired to endeavour his best to find out a fit man to supply that place of the Usher and present him to this House. And it is further ordered that Mr Laborne shall have forty shillings paid by the Chamberlains to him as a gratuity now at his departure. (24 January 1642) [9]

> Also this day Richard Orme, Master of Arts, is chosen to be Usher of the Free School of this town in the place of Mr Laborne, deceased, and is to have the same fee that Mr Laborne had. (10 July 1642) [10]

Most of the Ushers tended to stay for between three and six years. Hence Mr Orme was followed in the post of Usher by some nine others during Mr Bell's long period of service as Master. Edmund Keene (1648-51) was obviously well thought of as he was given a rise in salary in 1649:

> It is this day ordered that the Chamberlain shall pay to Mr Edmund Keene, Usher of the Free School, five pounds yearly from Our Lady [Day] last, in addition to his salary, that same payment to continue during the pleasure of this House. (5 May 1649) [11]

The Usher was not the only one to be given a rise. Two years later Mr Bell had his salary increased by 50%:

> It is this day ordered that Mr Edward Bell, Master of the Free School, shall have his 40 marks [£26 13s 4d] per annum made £40 per annum from Christmas last and to be paid by the Chamberlain during the pleasure of this house. (3 March 1651) [12]

As the Ushers left, often because they gained promotion in another school or a church living, it became the norm for the Corporation to ask Mr Bell to find someone to fill a vacancy by finding a suitable candidate as the Usher:

> Forasmuch as this House is informed that Mr Leeds, Usher of the Free School within this borough, is chosen to be Master of the Free School at Newark and there settled, and thereby the Free School within this town is at present void of an Usher in his place, and whereas Mr Edward Bell the Schoolmaster of the said school has this day informed this House that, according to their order, he has inquired and found out one Mr John Gibson, an able discreet person fit and qualified for the said employment, it is this day ordered that the said John Gibson be Usher of the said school under the said Master, Mr Edward Bell, to continue the same during the pleasure of this House, and that he have the same salary and allowances for the same as Mr Leeds, the said late Usher, formerly

had, he being diligent and faithful in his said place. (17 October 1659) [13]

As mentioned in Chapter 3 some of the Ushers had been pupils at the school before going to Cambridge. This was the case with James Hayes and Richard Nesling who had both been Titley Scholars at Emmanuel College:

> It is this day ordered that Richard Neslyn, Bachelor of Arts, shall be from this present day Usher of the Free School in the room and place of Mr James Haes, who has lately resigned up the said place, the same to commence from this present day and to be paid quarterly by the Chamberlains of this borough. (29 September 1670) [14]

> Whereas Mr Nesling has this day, by his letter to this House, declared that he is to serve at Houlton at Christmas next, therefore cannot attend the service of this town as Usher of the Grammar School, it is thereupon ordered that Mr Bell, Schoolmaster, do take care to provide another Usher in his room to be a while Usher upon liking before he be settled. (28 November 1673) [15]

The need for books for the Grammar School has been mentioned several times. In some cases helpful donations were made by local burgesses:

> This day by order of this House, forty shillings being paid into this House by several freeman towards the buying of necessary books for the public use of the Grammar School within this borough, was delivered into the hands of Mr Mayor to be paid to Mr Edward Bell, Master of the said Free School, for the purpose aforesaid. (8 August 1659) [16]

> This day 20s, paid into this House by Thomas Harriman for buying books for the Free School, was by order of this House paid into the hands of Mr Thomas Robinson, one of the Chamberlains, to be given unto Mr Edward Bell, the Master of the Free School, for the purpose above said. (12 May 1662) [17]

When he retired Mr Bell left a good number of books to his old school and the Corporation was duly grateful:

> This day Mr Edward Bell, late Master of the Grammar School, did present to the Mayor, Aldermen and Common Council of this borough twenty and six books, now being in the Grammar School, together with a small book being a catalogue of them, which this House do thankfully accept and do desire Mr Alderman Bell to return the thanks of this House to him accordingly. And it is this day ordered that a fair catalogue of the same books with the donor's name be made by the Town Clerk to be hung in the Grammar School. (18 December 1678) [18]

Earlier that year Mr John Horne was appointed as Mr Bell's successor and he was to be in post for some 52 years, an incredible length of time:

> This day Mr John Horne, Usher of the Free School of Norwich and Master of Arts, is chosen to be Master of the Grammar School, at £40 per annum salary, with free dwelling in the school house and also to receive similarly accustomed dues as Mr Bell used to receive, in case he shall accept, to enter at Midsummer next. (3 May 1678) [19]

John Horne had been born in Sutton St James in Lincolnshire but had been a pupil at the Grammar School in Lynn from which he had proceeded to Gonville and Caius College in Cambridge aged 14, taking his BA in 1662/3 and his MA in 1666.

Like many of the Schoolmasters before him and those to follow, John Horne was anxious to get the Corporation to carry out necessary repairs to his house and grounds:

> It is this day ordered that the Chamberlains do forthwith such repairs on the house of Mr Horne, being the school house, as shall appear to be necessary. (18 December 1678) [20]

This day Mr Holly, Mr Bell, Mr Robinson and Mr Evelyn, Aldermen, Mr Chennery, Mr Kidd, Mr Sparrow, Mr Ferrier and Mr Bell of the Common Council, or any three or more of them, whereof of one of the Aldermen aforesaid to be present, are desired to meet and to view and consider of a decayed wall on the west side of the schoolhouse garden and to search for such writings as concern the same so as it may be known at whose charge the same ought to be repaired, and to make report thereof to the next Hall. (13 June 1679) [21]

It is this day ordered that the wall on the west side of the ground belonging to the schoolhouse next [to] the ground now of Thomas Tue be forthwith repaired by the Chamberlains. (1 March 1680) [22]

Mr Horne was also very keen to get the school itself repaired. He wrote a series of plays, now lost, which was performed in the presence of the Mayor and Burgesses. His aim, according to L C Vernon, was to enlist 'the sympathies of the Borough authorities in his endeavours to repair the declining fortunes of the school.' Vernon, for many years the History Master at King Edward VII Grammar School, quotes the following somewhat purple passage from the Prologue to Horne's 1678 play as the introduction to an article in the school magazine in 1931:

Our orator was bound to recommend for your consideration the decaying condition of our School. A place beautiful for its structure, admirable for its uses and venerable for its antiquity, you are constituted her guardians by the charity of our pious ancestors. To you therefore she flies for protection in her distress and from your care she promises herself a ready supply of all her wants. Smooth her wrinkles, heal her wounds and suffer her not any longer to go clad in cobweb lawn.[23]

As we have seen, repairs to the house were carried out in 1678 and 1679 but the Hall Books contain no references to the school itself until 1687:

Mr Bell, Mr Pope, Mr Priest and Mr Bradfield of the Common Council are desired to inspect the wants of the Workhouse and the Free School and that William Bradford proceed to do such repairs as they shall judge needful. (14 October 1687) [24]

As in Mr Bell's time, Ushers came and went every few years. They were usually also offered the additional post of Library Keeper:

Also Mr Clement Scot, Master of Arts, late of Bennett College* in Cambridge, is this day chosen by this House to be Usher of the Grammar School, in the stead and room of Mr John Whiting. Also that he shall be the Library Keeper and that he shall be allowed the usual salary and other profits that Mr Whiting formerly had, during the good will and pleasure of this House. (20 April 1682) [25]

One person who remain Usher much longer than usual was Phillip Britiffe who was appointed in 1689 and left in 1715, both important dates in English History, although presumably neither the accession of William and Mary to the throne, nor the defeat of the Jacobites in Lancashire had any influence on the Grammar School in King's Lynn:

This day Mr Phillip Britiffe, Bachelor of Arts, is elected and chosen Usher of the Free School, during the pleasure of this House, and to have the usual salary of £21 per annum, to be paid him quarterly from Our Lady Day last.

Also he is appointed Keeper of the Library at St. Margaret's, during the pleasure as aforesaid, and to have 20s per annum salary to be paid him quarterly. (6 May 1689) [26]

Ordered that Mr Philip Britiffe, Usher of the Grammar School, at his own request be discharged, and his salary paid to this present Christmas. (21 December 1715) [27]

---

*Corpus Christi College

Over the years Mr Horne taught many boys who went on to university, including some who greatly distinguished themselves in their later careers. Among them were two brothers whose father, Charles Keene, was a mercer in King's Lynn and Mayor 1714-15. Benjamin Keene went up to Pembroke College, Cambridge, at 16 in 1713 and in 1718 gained the degree of Bachelor of Laws. He became an agent for the South Sea Company and British Consul in Madrid from 1724-27. As Minister Plenipotentiary to Spain 1727-39 and again 1748-1757, he negotiated the Treaty of Seville in 1729 and the Commercial Treaty of 1750 and was knighted in 1754. He died in Madrid in 1757 and is buried in St Nicholas Chapel in Lynn.

Benjamin's younger brother Edmund did not complete his school career at Lynn but transferred to Charterhouse in 1726 and it was from there that he went up to Gonville and Caius College in 1730. His career was to be mainly in the church but he was Master of Peterhouse in Cambridge from 1748 to 1754 and Vice Chancellor of the University from 1749 to 1751. In those days it was not unusual to hold more than one office, particularly an academic one and one in the church. However Edmund gave up his academic post not long after he was appointed Bishop of Chester in 1752, a position he held until 1771 when he became Bishop of Ely. He died in 1781 and was buried in Ely Cathedral.

It is Sir Benjamin Keene (Figure 11) after whom one of the four houses at King Edward VII Grammar School was named in 1923 when it was decided to replace North House, South House and Country House with the names of the two major benefactors, Thoresby and Lancaster, and that of one distinguished old boy. The name School House was retained for boarders.

Figure 11 Sir Benjamin Keene

Another of Lynn's famous sons, George Vancouver, is also believed to have been a pupil at the Grammar School under Mr Horne. John Jasper Vancouver was the Deputy Customs Officer for 22 years and the family lived in Fincham Street (today New Conduit Street). There were six children of whom George was the youngest. He joined the Royal Navy at 14 and sailed with Cook on both his second (1772-75) and third (1776-80) voyages. After nearly ten years in a number of different ships Captain Vancouver was appointed to lead what was to be a very successful expedition (1791-95) to survey the north–west coast of North America. Several places, including the largest city in British Columbia and Vancouver Island, bear his name.

In 1681, only three years after he took up his appointment as Master of the Grammar School, Mr Horne was made a Freeman of the town. He was clearly well regarded and this was still the case when he announced his intention of retiring. The Corporation decided to advertise widely in order to secure a satisfactory replacement:

> Ordered that Mr Underwood, the Town Clerk, do apply and consult with Alderman John Turner, Senior, at London about a proper Master for our Free School, which will be vacant at Lady Day next, the present Master having signified his intention of leaving the same by reason of his advanced age, and that he takes Alderman Turner's direction whether to insert the same in the London Gazette, or some other public newspaper, to give notice that any person properly qualified and well recommended may apply for the same, and to give notice of the endowment of the said school. (9 February 1730) [28]

> Ordered that at the request of Mr John Horne, Master of Arts and Master of the Free School of this borough, to be discharged from the Mastership, be discharged accordingly from Lady Day last.

> Ordered that thanks of this House be given to the said Mr Horne for his long and good service to the Mastership, as well by instilling good literature in the minds of the youth committed to his care, as by implanting good manners and the principles of religion on them.

> Ordered that Mr Alderman Bordman and Alderman Turner, Junior, attend the said Mr Horne and return the thanks of this House for his good service, together with Mr John Bagge and Mr Thomas Preston. (6 April 1730) [29]

Mr Horne did not survive long to enjoy retirement. He died, aged 90, in 1732 and was buried in St Nicholas Chapel.

Relations between the Corporation and some of John Horne's successors were not to be as easy as they had been with him and Mr Edward Bell as we shall see in the next chapter.

5. Some highs and lows of the Grammar School

John Horne's successor was Charles Squire (or Squires) who was the Schoolmaster from 1730 to 1739. Like his predecessor he too had been a pupil at the Lynn Grammar School from where he had gone up to Trinity College in Cambridge in 1713. He was awarded his BA in 1716/17, his MA in 1720 and was ordained a priest two years later.

> This day the Reverend Mr Charles Squires, Master of Arts, is chosen Master of the Grammar School, at the yearly salary of forty pounds, with free dwelling in the School House, and also to receive accustomed dues as his predecessor used to receive. (21 May 1730) [1]

Little is recorded in the Hall Books about his time as Schoolmaster, although we know that Mr Squires was assisted by the same Usher for much of the time he was in charge of the Grammar School:

> That the Reverend Robert Paine become Usher of the Grammar School at Lady Day next and receive the usual salary of an Usher there from that time. (21 December 1730) [2]

> Agreed that the Reverend Mr Robert Paine, Usher of the Grammar School, be and is hereby appointed Keeper of the Library in St Margaret's Church, and that the usual salary of forty shillings a year be allowed him from Lady Day last. (11 June 1732) [3]

Mackerell (1738) [4] described the Free School under Mr Squires as a large spacious building where the sons of Freemen of the town 'ought to be taught gratis, and be instructed in the Latin and Greek languages, until they be fit for some of our universities, or as long as the parents of the children shall think it.' The use of the word 'ought' suggests that this was not the case, an interpretation confirmed below. Mackerell also described the Schoolmaster's house, which he said was towards St James's End of the town, as having a very handsome brick front which was fitted up at the charge of the Corporation Anno 1646*, space for 'a great many boarders' and a large garden.

When the Reverend Robert Paine decided to leave in 1738 there was a dispute between the Corporation and the Schoolmaster about who should nominate a successor:

> Whereas the Reverend Mr Squires, Master of the Free Grammar School of this borough, hath pretended to an exclusive right of recommendation of an Usher to the election of the Mayor, Aldermen and Common Council, now it is agreed nemine contradicente [i.e. with no dissenting voices] that the right of electing an Usher of the Free Grammar School of this borough is in the Mayor, Aldermen and Common Council, and that no particular person has an exclusive right to recommend an Usher to the Mayor, Aldermen and Common Council's election.

> Agreed that the Reverend Mr John Wood, Bachelor of Arts, is by the whole House nominated and elected into the office of Usher of the Free Grammar School of this borough from Michaelmas next, at the yearly rate of twenty-two pounds, and as Keeper of the Library at St. Margaret's Parish Church, during the pleasure of this House. (29 August 1738) [5]

At the same Hall the Corporation insisted on the right of the Freemen of the borough to have their sons educated without charge at the Grammar School. This issue would be one that would re-occur several times in future years:

---

* This date is incorrect as the re-building of the Schoolmaster's house almost opposite the Greyfriars Tower, as we have seen, took place in 1659. The School was located in the former Charnel Chapel.

> Agreed that neither the Master nor the Usher for the time being has any right to claim any fee or gratuity upon the admission of the son of a Freeman into the said school or for his education during his continuance there. (29 August 1738) [5]

Possibly as a result of this spat with the Corporation Mr Squires decided to resign his post the following year. Clearly he did not need the position as he was also Rector at Little Massingham and at Congham, both of which livings he held until his death in 1752:

> This day the Reverend Mr Charles Squires personally appeared before this House and gave notice that he intended to resign the Mastership of the Free Grammar School of this borough at Midsummer next, and desired that the Mayor, Aldermen and Common Council of this borough would be pleased to provide a Master therefore accordingly. This House (accepting the notice of such resignation) have now nominated, chosen, elected and appointed and do nominate, choose, elect and appoint the Reverend Mr Thomas Pigge, clerk, AM[*1], to be Master of the said Grammar School at and from Midsummer next, with the usual salary and perquisites, during the pleasure of the Mayor, Aldermen and Common Council. (3 February 1739) [6]

Little is known of Mr Pigge's time as Schoolmaster or of his resignation or dismissal, but the Corporation was clearly unhappy with his term of office as demonstrated by the comments in the following letter to his successor in 1746. This extract is also very informative as to the salary and other benefits attached to the posts of Master and Usher:

> Ordered by this House that the Town Clerk write to the Reverend Mr John Daville at York to acquaint him that the Master of the Grammar School in Lynn is entitled to a clear salary of forty pounds per annum, a good house and garden worth twenty pounds per annum and capable of accommodating twenty boarders or more, that the Usher's salary is twenty-three pounds and forty shillings as Library Keeper, that the Master receives forty shillings per annum over and above his salary for every scholar who is not a Freeman's son and has by agreement with the Usher for the time being for many years past allowed him eight pounds per year on account of his care and trouble in teaching such unfree boys[*2] as are at his end of the school. And it is moreover customary (though not due of right) for most Freemen to make the Master some annual present while his children go to the school. That the usual price for the boarders is sixteen pounds per annum, besides forty shillings a year for schooling; that till within ten years the school has been in a very flourishing condition, though now at a low ebb for reasons Mr Daville will understand when he comes to Lynn; that as the Corporation are desirous to retrieve the former credit and reputation of the school and from the character they have heard of Mr Daville they think him a person likely to do it, they will leave it to him to name an Usher if he pleases, that he may have an opportunity of setting out at first and afterwards continuing the school in such a method as he himself shall approve of. (30 June 1746) [7]

John Daville was a student at Trinity College in Cambridge and graduated with a BA in 1736/37. He is known to have been the Master of Doncaster Grammar School from 1637 to 1643, after which he presumably took up a post in York. How he came to apply for the post in Lynn or how his services were solicited is not documented but, as the following extract shows, he was keen to ensure he did not suffer a financial loss by moving to Norfolk and to know that he would have a fairly free hand in bringing about the improvements required by the Corporation:

> Upon reading and consideration now had of Mr Daville's letter from York the seventh instant, it is agreed by the Mayor, Aldermen and Common Council to make him a present of twenty-five pounds in regard of the charge he will be at in removing from so great a distance, and of his taking upon

---

[*1]Master of Arts
[*2]That is the sons of those who were not Freemen

him the duty of the Usher as well as Master of the Grammar School for the first year, and that at the end thereof this House will appoint an Usher. And the Town Clerk is ordered to send Mr Daville a letter to this purpose.

Resolved by the Mayor, Aldermen and Common Council that in regard there are so few boys now at the Grammar School and will be still fewer (as the Master thereof informs them) at Michaelmas, there will be no occasion for an Usher from and after that time.

And the Town Clerk is ordered to give the Reverend Mr Rushbrook, the present Usher, immediate notice that Mr Daville, the succeeding Master, is to take upon him the care and charge of the whole school, and that the Mayor, Alderman and Common Council return their thanks to Mr Rushbrook for his care, diligence and faithful discharge in execution of his duty. (31 July 1746) [8]

Mr Rushbrook not only lost his post as Usher but also that of Library Keeper at St Margaret's Church and he was not to be paid until he handed over the library keys:

Agreed that the Reverend Mr Charles Phelps be Library Keeper at the yearly salary of forty shillings, and that no one be admitted to have a key there but the Library Keeper for the time being, and that the Reverend Mr Rushbrook deliver the said books to Mr Phelps, whereon the Chamberlain is to pay Mr Rushbrook's salary. (20 September 1746) [9]

Charles Phelps, a former Titley Scholar at Emmanuel College, had previously been appointed as Usher and Library Keeper in June 1742 but had given up both positions in December of that year because of ill-health.

At the Hall held on 20 September 1746 an important committee was set up to establish a set of rules for the school to ensure that the problems it had been experiencing over the previous ten years or so could be overcome. Both the new Schoolmaster and the Reverend Charles Phelps were included as members of the committee:

Agreed and ordered that Mr Mayor for the time being, or his Deputy, Alderman Allen, Alderman Bagge, Alderman Cary, Alderman Sommersby, Mr Preston, Mr Henry Goodwyn, the Town Clerk, the Reverends Mr Daville and Mr Phelps, or any five or more of them, whereof the Mayor or his Deputy to be one, they are hereby appointed a Committee to enquire what books belong to the Grammar School and to make a catalogue thereof, and also to peruse the statutes of the said school and to report at the next congregation their opinion of the expediency of the same and to prepare at the same time such further and other orders as they shall judge proper for the better rule and government of the said school. (20 September 1746) [9]

Although there is no further mention in the Hall Books of this enquiry the Borough Archives contain a very detailed document entitled *The Statutes, Rules and Orders of and for the Grammar School,* dated 1747 [10]. This document includes a version of the 1662 Rules [11] referred to in Chapter 2 (see Appendix 3) for the conduct of the pupils but also far more detail on what is expected of the Master and Usher and on the organisation of the school:

In the choice of Master, singular care and circumspection shall be used that he be of healthful constitution and of exemplary life and conversation; pious, sober, grave, diligent, industrious, of authority to encourage virtue and discourage vice. He shall be excellently skilled in the Latin and Greek tongues and all niceties of both; a man dextrous in teaching; of temper and moderation, rather by fair means persuading to learning and goodness than forcing by severity; and of discretion wisely to distinguish between defects of nature and wilful negligence; such a Master shall be treated with all respect and encouragement.

The Usher shall, as near as may, be qualified like the Master.

When either Master or Usher shall be admitted all statutes concerning their office and charge shall be read and they shall subscribe to them with promise to observe them.

The Master and Usher shall instruct in good manners as well as literature and teach poor men's children with as much care and diligence as the rich.

They shall teach all Townsmen's* children gratis yet may receive what is voluntarily proffered. [*A note in the margin corrects this to 'Freemen's only']

The Usher shall teach by discretion and appointment of the Master.

Besides the usual performances of the school the Master shall yearly at Christmas, Easter and Whitsuntide appoint to every form particular exercises to be recited publicly before the Mayor, Aldermen and Common Council and, upon recital of these exercises before Easter, he shall give as an Honorary a book to each of the best performers in the two highest forms in the Upper end and in the highest form in the Lower end, still taking care that the best books be impartially bestowed upon the best merit. The three books shall be provided by the Master suiting the capacities of the several forms at the charge of the Corporation not exceeding the price of (blank) a book.

The Master and Usher shall not both at one time be absent from school unless for an hour or two at most and that upon extraordinary occasion; nor shall either of them be out of the town the whole year unless in time of vacation above ten days to be accounted jointly and severally, except upon very urgent occasion to be allowed by the Mayor, Aldermen and Common Council.

The Usher shall yearly the week after Easter and Michaelmas deliver to the Mayor, Aldermen and Common Council in writing a perfect list containing the names of all the scholars of the school, distinguishing those who are new ones within the preceding half year.

Neither Master nor Usher shall have any benefice with care of souls nor any other employment which may hinder their continual and diligent attendance at school.

Neither Master nor Usher shall haunt taverns, alehouses, gaming houses or houses of infamy.

If any contention shall happen between the Master and Usher, the Mayor, Aldermen and Common Council shall determine it. In case either party shall refuse the determination, he shall be expelled the school.

Both Master and Usher, in case of evil conversation, neglect the school or breach the statutes, may after two admonitions of the Mayor, Aldermen and Common Council be removed, yet not withstanding three months warning.

So some fairly strict conditions of service were to be introduced by these new statutes. The fact that such vices as drink, gambling and whoring were forbidden suggests that there had been such instances in the past. Similarly the fact that Mr Squires and Mr Pigge had held benefices had highlighted the problem of neglect of the school.

The rules concerning the organisation and curriculum give us an interesting insight into school life in the middle of the eighteenth century:

Times of vacation shall be these and none other: from O Sapientia, being the 16th of December, till Monday after Epiphany commonly called Plough Monday; Monday and Tuesday next before Ash Wednesday; from Thursday next before Easter and Whitsuntide respectively till Monday sennight [seven nights later] respectively; following all church holidays, all days of public humiliation and thanksgivings; and Saturday in the afternoon.

The Usher shall take care that the school, with all things in it and belonging to it, shall be kept clear and in order.

The Usher shall take care that the school doors be opened every morning and afternoon to let the scholars in and shut always when the school is done.

Every school day between the twenty-ninth day of September and the twenty-fifth day of March, the Usher shall be at school by seven o'clock in the morning; and from the twenty-fifth day of March to the twenty-ninth day of September he shall be there by six. He shall stay there always till eleven. By one o'clock, after dinner he shall return and there continue until five.

The Master shall every morning from the twenty-ninth day of September and the twenty-fifth day of March, be at school within half an hour after seven; and from the twenty-fifth day of March to the twenty-ninth day of September he shall be there within half an hour after six. He shall continue there till half an hour after ten; at one he shall be there again and remain till five. And let the Master and Usher diligently apply themselves in instructing the scholars under their respective care during those school hours.

All scholars shall follow the same hours which are enjoyed by the Usher.

The whole school shall consist of seven forms, whereof four shall be in the lower end. The highest form of the low end shall every year after Christmas be taken up to the high end. And then the second form of the high end shall be joined to the highest form, such scholars being left behind as the Master shall not think fit to advance.

One very surprising piece of information to be gleaned from the 1747 Statutes is that there were to be seven forms yet there were only two teachers. The forms must have been relatively small groupings of boys of different ages/abilities, all taught within the same room.

Some of the books to be used were laid down in the statutes, although there was no prescription as to which would be used by particular forms, and other books, except those which were 'barbarous', were permitted:

Every form shall learn such of the following books as may best suit their several capacities and such as the Master shall judge proper….and such others as are composed with solid judgement and brisk and lively fancy, such as promote virtue, such as express the strength and purity of language, declare the ancient Greek and Roman customs and inform the scholar in poetic fictions. Barbarous books shall be wholly excluded and all obscene passages in what author so ever omitted.

The Master and Usher shall often admonish their scholars to speak Latin both in school and out of it.

Besides the English catechism nothing shall be taught in the school but Latin and Greek.

The Master and Usher shall take great care that all their scholars read and pronounce articulately with proper sound and accent, that they well understand their lectures and know what phrases are in them, what tropes and figures and what also remarkable, and repeat deliberately and perfectly what book is requisite.

On Fridays account shall be taken of all lectures in the foregoing week or so much of them as the Master shall find convenient.

Account shall be taken by the Master and Usher of all offences against any statute, or against piety and good manners, and punishment shall be inflicted accordingly, regard being always had that more favour be shown to such as offend but seldom and through infirmity than to frequent and obstinate offenders.

There is a long list of possible offences such as appear in the 1662 Rules with some additions, such as breaking of windows. Similarly there are rules for the Master and Usher regarding teaching:

Let the masters deliver whatever their scholars are to be taught in a clear and obvious manner first explaining those things with many examples; let them never take out a new lesson till they thoroughly have comprehended their old one; for it matters not how soon but how well, nor to read many things, but to understand what you read.

The Minister at St Margaret's Church and the Lecturer at St Nicholas Chapel were to examine the scholars every year in the week before the Feast of John the Baptist (24 June) and report back to the Mayor and Burgesses.

This was indeed a very comprehensive set of rules and regulations for the conduct of all aspects of the Grammar School!

The physical condition of the Grammar School, as well as its spiritual, moral and academic wellbeing was also to be given detailed consideration by the special committee appointed by the Corporation:

Agreed by this House that the gentlemen on the Grammar School Committee, or any five or more of them of whom the Mayor or his Deputy to be one, be and they are desired to survey the said school in order to see what repairs are wanting to be done thereto, and to make an estimate of what it will cost to repair the same and to make report thereof the next Hall Day. (29 August 1747) [12]

Whereas at a congregation held the 29th day of August last the gentlemen on the Grammar School Committee were desired to survey the said school and report what repairs are wanting to be done thereto, and to estimate the charges to repair the same, now the said Committee do report that upon their view and other information the south gutter and tiling on both sides of the said school and glazing are in bad repair but that the north gutter appears to be in good condition. That the glaziers' work will cost nine pounds to put the windows and the lantern in good repair and that it will amount to thirty pounds to new tile the school and repair the gutters, still liable to frequent reparations from the narrowness of these gutters within the parapet wall, these gutters being by no means properly laid to carry the waters. But to remedy that this Committee recommend to this House the parapet and leaden gutters on both sides be taken away and the walls lowered to such a slope as to lie fair to be tiled over to meet the roof, by which means the water will be carried off by dripping, and the lead of the gutters may be sold, which they expect will save ten pounds, so that the school may be new tiled for about ten pounds inclusive of the said lead. And the Committee do further report that the roof of the school is of good oak and in substantial repair and that mending the floor and the forms and whiting the school may cost about five pounds more. So that if this method is approved of by this House the whole school, within and without, may be put into a thorough repair for about twenty-four or twenty-five pounds charge to the Corporation. Now the Mayor, Aldermen and Common Council, having duly weighed the contents of the said report, do agree hereto and order that the several works therein mentioned be proceeded upon and finished in such a manner as is hereby recommended with all convenient speed by the Chamberlain, under the direction of Alderman Allen, Alderman Bagge, Alderman Sommersby or any two of them. (29 September 1747) [13]

Clearly a considerable amount of work was needed on the Old Charnel Chapel. At the same Hall it was agreed that an Usher should be appointed once again:

Resolved by this House that for the credit and increase of their Grammar School there shall be an Usher and that a proper person for that office be forthwith enquired after by Mr Daville or any gentleman of the Hall. And Mr Daville is desired to continue his care of the whole school whose extraordinary trouble shall be considered and rewarded until an Usher is provided. (29 September 1747) [13]

The Corporation was clearly pleased with the progress of the Grammar School under Mr Daville as he was made a Freeman in March 1748:

The Reverend John Daville, clerk, and the Reverend Charles Phelps, clerk, who[se] freedoms were voted at the Hall, appearing did severally take the usual oaths and sound pledges. (7 March 1748) [14]

Later that year an Usher was appointed to assist Mr Daville, but it was not until 1753 that he was awarded an addition to his salary to compensate him for the time when he had managed without one:

Agreed by the Mayor, Aldermen and Common Council that Mr Thomas Hutchinson be and is now appointed Usher of the Grammar School for one year from the twenty-fifth day of December instant, at the salary of twenty-three pounds. And that Mr Daville do at his option either pay the Usher eight pounds per annum or allow him the benefit of all the unfree boys at his end of the school according to ancient custom. (23 December 1748) [15]

Ordered by the Mayor, Aldermen and Common Council that the Chamberlain pay Mr Daville, Master of the Grammar School, twenty guineas for his officiating as Usher there for five quarters of a year from Michaelmas 1747 to Christmas 1748. (23 July 1753) [16]

Yet more work was done on the school in 1752 when it was agreed that a new chimney should be built which would allow coal to be burned instead of charcoal:

Mr Daville, Master of the Grammar School, having desired that a chimney might be built in the school for the burning of sea coals instead of charcoal there, and the Chamberlain having been ordered to make an estimate of making such a chimney, and the Chamberlain now reporting to the Mayor, Aldermen and Common Council that a chimney on one side of the said school and a stove iron grate for the burning of sea coals may be built and made at a charge to the Mayor and Burgesses not exceeding six pounds, it is now ordered that the Chamberlain cause such chimney and fire grate made and fixed in the said school with all convenient speed, at a charge not exceeding that sum. (20 November 1752) [17]

Mr Daville resigned his post as Schoolmaster in 1755 and took up two Norfolk livings, the first as Vicar of Islington and the second as Vicar of Wiggenhall St Mary. In 1765 he also became Rector of Boughton. He held all three livings until his death in 1800.

Despite the new rules and the obvious regard in which John Daville had been held the numbers in the school were again very low when a new Master was being sought in April 1755 and the Usher was given notice to leave:

This House being informed that there now are, and have been for some time past, no more than three boys at both ends of the Grammar School here, the Mayor, Aldermen and Common Council are of the opinion, nemine contradicente, that there is no occasion for an Usher in so declined a state. However they are pleased to order that the Town Clerk signify to the Reverend Thomas Hutcheson that his office as Usher of the said school shall be continued to him until Michaelmas next when it is to determine. (24 April 1755) [18]

However not long after the new Schoolmaster, John Knox (1755-1760), was appointed he asked for the help of an Usher because of ill health:

The letter from Mr Knox, Master of the Grammar School, dated the twentieth instant, addressed to the Mayor, was read, setting forth that he is in a bad state of health and apprehensive that his health will not be so far confirmed for some time to enable him to take pains with his pupils that he desires to do, more especially as they are likely to be more numerous after the holidays, and therefore praying that Mr Mayor will please to move this House to allow him an Usher. Now the motion being put it is agreed that the Mayor, Aldermen and Common Council, for the reasons assigned in Mr Knox's letter, to allow him an Usher to be by them approved of. And it is hereby ordered that Mr Knox do enquire after and propose to this House a layman for officiating as Usher of the said school subject to their approbation. (22 December 1755) [19]

The last two appointments of Ushers to be reported in the Hall Books come in the next few years and both proved to be unsatisfactory ones. Mr Birkes was dismissed after little more than a year:

> Mr John Knox, having informed this house that he has procured Mr John Birkes as his Usher in the Grammar School, the said John Birkes is hereby approved of, to remain in that place during the pleasure and under the control and power entirely of the said Mr Knox; and it is further ordered that the Usher's salary be paid to the said Mr Knox from Michaelmas last and continued during the pleasure of this House. (29 September 1756) [20]

> Mr Knox having informed this House by letter that he had dismissed John Birkes, his late Usher, and had engaged Eugenius Aram in his stead, subject to their approbation, the said Eugenius Aram is approved of by this House during the pleasure and under the control and power entirely of the said Mr Knox. And it is ordered that the Usher's salary be paid to Mr Knox during the pleasure of this House. (14 February 1758) [21]

Although he had had no formal education and was certainly not a university graduate, as had been most of his predecessors, Aram had taught in a number of schools in London before obtaining the appointment of Usher in King's Lynn. It would seem that he had a knowledge of Latin and Greek and the manners of a gentleman. However he was not to be long at the Grammar School. Eugene Aram (Figure 12) was arrested, after only a few months in the post, for a murder which had been committed some fourteen years previously. After a celebrated trial in York, Aram was found guilty and was hanged in 1759. There is an exhibition in the Old Gaol House Museum in King's Lynn, which describes the details of the murder and the trial. Aram's skull and a part of the skull of his victim, Daniel Clarke, are on display. Much has been written on the subject, including Thomas Hood's dramatic narrative poem, *The Dream of Eugene Aram*,

Figure 12 Eugene Aram, Usher of the Grammar School in 1758

(1829), a novel, *Eugene Aram* by Edward Bulwer-Lytton (1832) and an appraisal of the facts of the case, *Eugene Aram, His Life and Trial* by E R Watson (1913). As late as the 1950s the case was the subject of an article in the Annals of the Royal College of Surgeons of England from which the picture of Eugene Aram is taken. [22]

As we have seen the teaching to this point had taken place in the former Charnel Chapel building. However at about the time of Eugene Aram's arrest in 1758 Mr Knox is given permission to teach the boys in his own house in St James Street:

> Agreed that Mr John Knox, Master of the Grammar School, may teach his scholars at the house he now lives in. And it is ordered that the Chamberlain provide proper forms and tables for that purpose, and also that the garden ground be cleared and laid down at a charge not exceeding five pounds in the whole. (29 September 1758) [23]

Although the Hall Books make no reference to the court case or Mr Aram's departure there is an entry in which the concern of the Corporation about the Grammar School is obvious:

> The Mayor and Mr Recorder are desired by the Aldermen and Common Council to enquire into the management of the Grammar School here and consult about getting a proper Usher for the same and to report in writing the result of their enquiry of consultation to this House at their next assembly. (14 February 1760) [24]

Despite this no further references to the appointment of Ushers have been found and it would seem that from this date the Schoolmaster received the allowance of £23 per year and was responsible for employing his own Usher. Nor does any report on the management of the Grammar School appear in the Hall Books in this period.

Perhaps because of the scandal caused by the conviction of Eugene Aram and the opprobrium attached to the Grammar School, Mr Knox left his post in 1760. However no blame seems to have been laid at Mr Knox's door as he was given an open testimonial by the Corporation and appointed Master of the Grammar School in Holt:

> The Mayor, Aldermen and Common Council do hereby certify by their Town Clerk that Mr John Knox was accepted and admitted Master of the Grammar School here at Michaelmas 1755 upon the recommended of personages of character who had entrusted to him the education of their children, and that he has continued Master of this school ever since and discharged his trust to the satisfaction of those gentlemen who have committed their children to his care. (21 July 1760) [25]

> Mr Mayor now brought in a letter addressed to this House from Mr John Knox, Master of the Grammar School here, informing them that he was elected Master of the Grammar school at Holt on the twenty-third of last month, whereupon Mr David Lloyd is by the Mayor, Aldermen and Common Council elected Master of the Free Grammar School of this borough in the said Mr Knox's room to have the messuage, called the school house, rent free and the usual salary, during their pleasure. (29 September 1760) [26]

David Lloyd was to hold the post of Master for some 34 years and became highly regarded by the Corporation as we shall see in the next chapter.

6. Changing locations of the Grammar School

During the Mastership of David Lloyd, an Oxford graduate, the old school building was replaced but the information available about the use of the old Charnel Chapel is somewhat conflicting. The Reverend Edward Edwards was a boy at the Grammar School from 1772 to 1778, and his widely-produced sketch of the old school is shown in Figure 13. However the building was demolished in 1779 and Edwards drew the sketch from memory some years later. An etching based on Edwards's sketch appears in William Taylor's *Antiquities of Lynn* published in 1844 [1] and Taylor refers to it as 'probably the only memorial of the chapel now in existence.' Taylor does however also refer to Henry Bell's partial drawing, of about 1675, showing that the Grammar School was separated from the north-west corner of the church, not attached to it (Figure 14). In his writing on the buildings of Lynn, Henry Bell makes the location clear: 'Adjoining to the north-west corner of the church [St Margaret's] is a very handsome free grammar school with neat lanthorn in the middle of it.' [2] Much later E M Beloe (1899) [3] also points out the inaccuracy of Edwards's drawing and in a sketch of his own shows what he believes to be the accurate location of the former Charnel Chapel in relation to St Margaret's Church (Figure 15).

Presumably Edwards was taught in the old Charnel Chapel building as shown in his sketch. As we have seen, Mr Knox had been given leave to teach the boys in his own house in 1758 and the Corporation had agreed to provide 'proper forms and tables for that purpose'. However the Hall Book entries in the 1760s suggest that the teaching is once again in the school building since the following entries make a distinction between the Grammar School and the school house:

Figure 13 The Grammar School by the Reverend Edward Edwards

Agreed that Mr Mayor and his Deputy, Alderman Sommersby, Alderman Charles Turner, Mr Hamilton, Mr Elsden and Mr Maxey Allen, or any two or more of them, whereof Mr Mayor or his Deputy to be one, be and they are hereby appointed a Committee to give directions for erecting a necessary house [lavatory] for the scholars of the Free Grammar School, and also to cause such repairs to be done to the Master's house as they shall judge proper, so as such repairs do not exceed the sum of fifteen pounds. (28 June 1762) [4]

Ordered that the Chamberlain cause writing forms or desks to be made at the Grammar School and do such repairs as are wanting at the school house so that the same exceed not in the whole the sum of ten pounds. (29 August 1765) [5]

Figure 14 Henry Bell's sketch of St Margaret's Church and the Grammar School in about 1675

In 1770 there are a number of entries which refer to the building of additional accommodation at the Schoolmaster's house:

Ordered that a building be erected, at the expense of this Corporation, with Ely brick and fir timber on the piece of ground to be taken in exchange from Mr Edward Everard, adjoining to the Grammar School house, of the following dimensions viz. the length from east to west of the whole piece of ground purchased, twenty foot wide and the height of the present roof of the Grammar School house, so that lodging rooms may be made over the room which the boys are to play and dine in if this House shall afterwards think proper. And it is further ordered that the Chamberlain do make out the dimensions and scantlings of the said intended building, one as a room only for the boys to play and dine in, and the other as such a room with lodging rooms over it, and deliver the same to several workmen in the town for their delivering in estimates sealed up at what prices they will do the whole

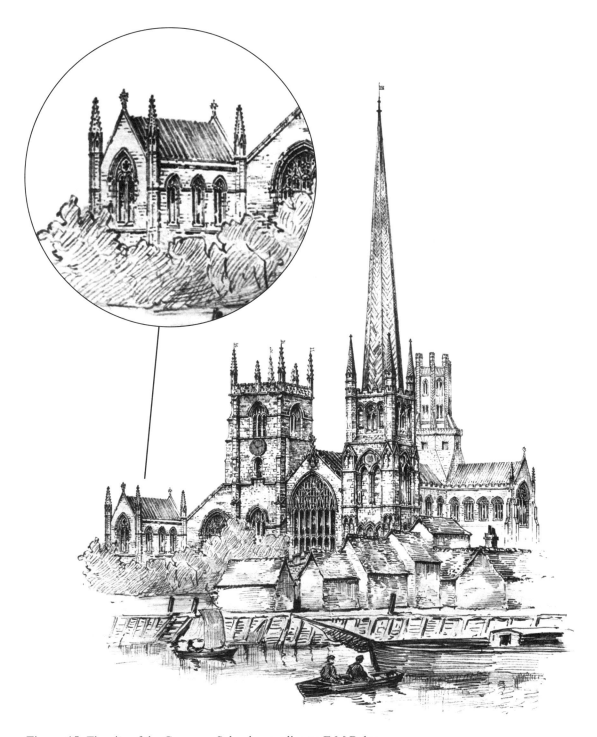

Figure 15 The site of the Grammar School according to E M Beloe

of each of the said works and finish the same, to be considered at the next Hall. (2 July 1770) [6]

Ordered by this House that a school room, for the use of the Grammar Schoolmaster for the time being, be erected at the expense of this Corporation on the piece of ground to be taken in exchange from Mr Edward Everard, adjoining the Grammar School House, agreeable to the plan and elevation of No. 5 delivered in by the Chamberlain to this Corporation, with the remarks and elevations in the margin of the said plan. And it is agreed by this House that the Mayor and his Deputy and the rest of the members of this House or any five or more of them, whereof the Mayor or his Deputy to be one, be and they are hereby appointed a Committee to agree with any workmen that are willing to execute such building with Ely bricks and other proper materials as in a former order agreeable to the plan of No. 5 under the inspection of the Chamberlain, and that such workmen do execute an agreement with this Corporation for completing such building. (27 July 1770) [7]

Although the last entry refers to a school room it is unlikely that it was intended for teaching, rather that it was a room for the scholars to dine and play in as indicated in the entry of 2 July. In any event the building goes ahead later that year:

Agreed that William Tuck, carpenter, do build the Grammar School room in a workmanlike manner, of the dimensions and of the materials he has agreed with the Chamberlain, to do the same as appears by the plan and particulars this day signed by them and left with the Chamberlain. And it is ordered that he be paid for the same the sum of three hundred and twenty-five pounds. (22 September 1770) [8]

Three years later further improvements and alterations are made to the house in St James Street:

It was agreed that Mr David Lloyd, the Master of the Grammar School, be allowed by this Corporation the sum of twenty pounds for building a new staircase and making other alterations in the Grammar School house, the sum to be paid to him by the Chamberlain when the work is properly done. (4 June 1773) [9]

It is possible that the state of the old Grammar School building was such that the teaching did at this stage take place in St James Street, because by the end of the decade the former Charnel Chapel was pulled down to make way for a new Butchers' Shambles, the old one also being demolished. A number of plans had been considered but in July 1779 agreement was reached to build the new Shambles 'with school rooms over them':

This day the Chamberlain brought in a model and plan for new Shambles in the Saturday Market, with school rooms over them, which being approved by this House, it is now resolved and ordered that the former plan of building them be laid aside and the present adopted, and therefore it is agreed that Mr Mayor and the rest of the Hall or any five or more of them, who shall meet on Mr Mayor's summons (whereof the Mayor for the time being or his Deputy be one) be and they are hereby appointed a Committee to contract and agree with such person or persons as they shall think proper for erecting and building Shambles, with school rooms over them, according to the said model and plan now brought in. And it is further agreed and ordered that such Shambles and school rooms be built upon the ground where the old Grammar School now stands, or as near thereto as may be, and that the said Grammar School be taken down also at the expense of this Corporation. (5 July 1779) [10]

The new Butchers' Shambles (Figure 16) was completed and insured by 1780 as shown by the following extract and it seems clear that at this stage the teaching took place in a room in this building:

Agreed that the sum of one thousand pounds be insured by the Chamberlain in the Royal Exchange Assurance office on the now erected Shambles and Schools over the same in Saturday Market and the sum of one thousand pounds on the Cross and Shambles in Tuesday Market Place. (21 December 1780) [11]

In 1783 Charles Phelps, the former Grammar school scholar, who had been appointed Librarian to the Corporation in 1746 died and David Lloyd took on this extra role:

This day it is agreed that Mr David Lloyd, Master of the Grammar School, be Librarian to this

Corporation in [the] stead of the Revd Mr Charles Phelps, deceased, at the yearly salary of forty shillings, he delivering to Mr Mayor at next Hall, or in a month, a catalogue of the books now in the Library with his remarks thereon, and that he do yearly on the fourteenth day of February deliver unto this House a catalogue of the books. (14 February 1783) [12]

A year later the Schoolmaster was made a Freeman in recognition of his services to Lynn and the award of a doctorate by the University of Oxford:

The Freedom of this Borough is this day granted gratis to David Lloyd, Doctor of Laws of the University of Oxford, he having been Master of the Grammar School of this town for twenty-four years last past, and he appearing took the usual oaths and Oath of Freedom and found pledges for his good behaviour. (4 June 1784) [13]

Note: For no given reason, he and one other tendered their resignations as Freemen on 2 August and this was accepted but at the next Hall on 11 August the decision was revoked.

Dr Lloyd died in 1794 and was succeeded, albeit for only three years, by his son, Henry Lloyd, who had gone up to Trinity College, Cambridge, in 1781 and had been made a Fellow in 1787. As we saw in Chapter 3, although he was clearly not a 'poor scholar', when he went up to Cambridge from the Grammar School he had been granted both the Peirson's and Hall's Exhibitions, each of 40s per year.

Whether any other candidates for the post were considered is not known. However being Dr Lloyd's son, a former pupil of the Grammar School and an academic of some standing, Henry Lloyd would have been seen as an ideal candidate for the post of Schoolmaster:

Figure 16 The Shambles on Saturday Market Place (demolished in 1914)

The Mayor, Aldermen and Common Council do this day unanimously elect and appoint the Reverend Henry Lloyd, Master of Arts and Fellow of Trinity College in the University of Cambridge, to be Master of the Free Grammar School of this borough in the room of Dr David Lloyd, his father deceased, late Master thereof, to hold such Mastership during the pleasure of the Mayor, Aldermen and Common Council, at the salary of forty pounds per annum, besides the use of the school rooms and of the dwelling house with the yard, garden and appurtenances and other accustomed privileges, and the further annual allowance of twenty three pounds for a suitable Usher whom the said Henry Lloyd hath, with the consent of this House, undertaken to provide for his assistance within the said school. (22 December 1794) [14]

What is surprising is that Henry Lloyd accepted the post. His letter of resignation in 1797 is preserved in the Borough Archives [15]. In it he refers to 'the superior comforts and advantages to be enjoyed in the University of Cambridge' and to the fact that he found himself 'incapable of confirming' his 'exertions in such a manner as may be satisfactory' to the Corporation or to himself. It is clear that he could not devote his full attention to the school since he had been appointed Regius Professor of Hebrew in 1795, a post he held until his death in 1831. The year after leaving Lynn he also became Vicar of Babraham in Cambridge.

In both the entry above, ratifying Henry Lloyd's appointment, and that referring to the appointment of his successor, the Reverend Richard Scott (1797 to 1803) the phrase 'the use of the school rooms and of the dwelling house' is used, so there is little doubt that the teaching took place in the school room above the Shambles and not in the Schoolmaster's house. Little is known of the Grammar School under the Reverend Scott or about the period under his successor, the Reverend Martin Coulcher (1803-1818), except that numbers were relatively small. What we do know is that moves were afoot which were to lead to the Grammar School moving out of the Shambles. In 1815 there is a proposal to use a room next to the school room as a library:

It being represented to this House that the Public Subscription Library which was established in this town in or about the year 1797 containing a great number of valuable books and that it would much contribute to the success of that establishment if the Corporation were to grant to the subscribers to the said library the use of the vacant room at the west end of the School over the Saturday Market butchery, and would add to it the books belonging to the Corporation which are in the library belonging to St Margaret's Church. Resolved that it be referred to the Committee for General Purposes together with the Reverend Stephen Allen, Librarian, the Reverend Edward Edwards, Lecturer, and the Reverend Martin Coulcher, Master of the Grammar School, (who are requested to give their assistance) to enquire into the propriety of such a measure, and to report their opinion thereon to this House on Michaelmas Day next. (29 August 1815) [16]

It was not until 1818 that the Mayor was given permission for the vacant room to be used as a subscription room. However it is not clear whether this was to be as a library or for other purposes:

Agreed that the Mayor be empowered to grant leave during [his] pleasure for the use of the vacant room adjoining the Grammar school as a subscription room to be maintained as such by a society of gentlemen now formed; and with power for the subscribers to make, at their own expense, any necessary alterations and improvements in the room. (14 February 1818) [17]

Martin Coulcher died in May 1818 but a few months earlier he arranged for his son to be awarded one of the two Titley Scholarships:

Agreed that Wiliam Bedell Coulcher, now or late a scholar educated in the Grammar School of this town, be and is hereby nominated and recommended to one of the vacant Scholarships or

Exhibitions called Lynn Scholarships or Mr Titley's Scholarships in Emmanuel College in the University of Cambridge, with the benefits, stipends and privileges appertaining. (14 February 1818) [17]

The son of his successor, the Reverend Thomas Kidd (1818-25) was also to be nominated for a scholarship at Emmanuel:

> The Mayor, Aldermen and Common Council do this day nominate and recommend Richard Bentley Porson Kidd, late scholar of the Grammar School of this borough, to one of the places or preferments called Lynn Scholarships or Mr Titley's Scholarships in Emmanuel College in the University of Cambridge, with all the benefits, stipends and privileges appertaining to the said scholarship. (13 February 1826) [18]

Numbers of pupils at the Grammar School must have increased at the beginning of Thomas Kidd's time as Master since he asked and was granted permission to use a second room over the Shambles in April 1820:

> A letter from the Revd Thomas Kidd, Master of the Grammar School, dated the second day of February last, applying for the room now used as a subscription room to be added to his school room over the Shambles, being now read; ordered that it be communicated to Mr Kidd, in answer to his letter, that the Corporation will give directions for their resuming possession of the room and for accommodating Mr Kidd with the same, as soon as convenient; it being understood that a proviso was made to Mr Kidd of this accommodation when wanted, although it appears by the Corporation Books that this room was not originally attached to the Grammar school. (24 April 1820) [19]

This decision seems to have prompted a major new initiative. Later that year an important proposal was considered by the Corporation which soon led to the school being located in St James Street by the Schoolmaster's house:

> A proposal having been made to the Corporation by several gentlemen of the town for buying a piece of ground next [to] the Grammar School play ground, near Saint James Street, and building thereon two new school rooms, similar to or as large in extent as the two rooms over the Shambles in the Saturday Market Place, (one of which rooms is now used as the School Room attached to the Grammar School) and making those new buildings to be part of the Grammar School establishment, by way of exchange for a lease from the Corporation of those rooms over the Shambles for ninety nine years, at a nominal rent, to be used as a Library, or as reading or subscription rooms…. And the plan having been communicated to the Reverend Thomas Kidd, the Master of the Grammar School, and having received his approbation: Resolved that the proposal above mentioned has the approbation and concurrence of this Corporation and that it be referred to the Committee for General Purposes to settle the detail of the plan and the precise terms of the lease and covenant on both sides. (3 November 1820) [20]

On 11 December 1820, the Committee examined the plan and specification for the new school rooms to be built and attached to the grammar school and resolved 'that the building be erected at the proper season of the next year, upon the plan proposed'. As the following extract from the Hall Book makes clear, the Grammar School had moved from the room above the Shambles and was located in the new school room in St James Street by the middle of 1822:

> Agreed that the question in relation to repairs of the room in Saturday Market Place lately occupied by the Revd Thomas Kidd as a Grammar School be referred to the consideration and direction of the House Committee. (29 August 1822) [21]

In 1825 Thomas Kidd left Lynn and later held the posts of Schoolmaster at both Wymondham School and Norwich Grammar School, as well as holding various livings in Norfolk, including

Bedingham, Croxton and Eltisley. His son Richard mentioned above, was named Richard Porson after the celebrated classical scholar of that name, with whom Thomas Kidd had become acquainted at Cambridge.

The Reverend John Bransby was to be the Schoolmaster for the next twenty five years. He was to become a thorn in the side of the Corporation and as a result the Town Clerk, Frederick Lane, produced reports in February 1836 and again in May 1836 on the origins of the school and also concerning the rights and privileges of the Schoolmaster. Legal advice was sought and a great deal of money expended as we shall see in the next chapter.

7. The Reverend John Bransby (1825 to 1850)

John Bransby (Figure 17) was a graduate of St John's College, Cambridge. He took his BA in 1805, MA in 1808 and was ordained a priest in 1807. In about 1806 he is believed to have started a school in Stoke Newington in Middlesex at which the celebrated American poet, Edgar Allan Poe, was a pupil. It is also said that he was the prototype of William Wilson in the Poe story of the same name. His time as Master of the Grammar School in Lynn was certainly a bit of a saga.

The full entry recording Bransby's appointment is reproduced below since the terms on which he was appointed were to be contested hotly in the 1830s and 1840s:

> The Mayor, Aldermen and Common Council do this day unanimously elect and appoint the Reverend John Bransby, Master of Arts, late of St John's College in the University of Cambridge, to be Master of the Free Grammar School within this borough, in the place and on resignation of the Reverend Thomas Kidd, to hold the said Mastership from the twenty-fourth day of June instant, during the pleasure of the Mayor, Aldermen and Common Council, at a salary of forty pounds per annum, besides the use of the present School Rooms and of the dwelling house with the yards, garden and other appurtenances, and other accustomed privileges, and at a further allowance of twenty-three pounds per annum for a suitable Usher, whom the said John Bransby, with the consent of this Hall, is to undertake to provide and constantly employ for his assistance in the proper tuition of the pupils within the said school. (13 June 1825) [1]

Following the building of the new school room in 1821-22 it was decided that important work also needed to be carried out on the Grammar School house:

> Agreed that it be referred to the House Committee to examine the state of the Grammar School buildings, and of the Master's dwelling house and to order the necessary repairs to be done under their direction. (13 June 1825) [1]

The report dated the fourth day of July instant of the House Committee respecting the Grammar school being now read:

> Agreed that it be referred to the House Committee to determine upon and carry into execution a plan for pulling down the Grammar School dwelling house, either wholly or in part, and for rebuilding the same. And that the money required for

Figure 17 The Reverend John Bransby (from an oil painting by John Rutland)

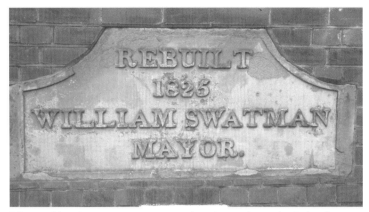

Figure 18 The stone commemorating the work on the School house in 1825

Figure 19 The entrance to the Grammar School in St James Street

executing the work be raised by the grant of annuities to be secured by bonds from this Corporation. (8 July 1825) [2]

The latter entry is highly significant since it was to result in the second major re-building of the Schoolmaster's house, commemorated by a stone which included the name of the Mayor, William Swatman and the date, 1825 (Figure 18). This stone, along with the one from the time of Edward Bell, was fixed above the main entrance. Today those two stones, but not a third which can be seen in Figure 19, showing the Lynn crest, were fixed into the wall on either side of the main entrance of King Edward Vll School in 1939 (Figure 20).

Various meetings of the Committee were held in July and August. On 21 July a plan was agreed and estimates were invited and on 15 August it was decided that the lowest of the three estimates, £1320, would be recommended to the next Hall for ratification:

Resolved that the order of the Committee in reference to making a contract for building a new Grammar school dwelling house be, and the same is hereby confirmed, and the Mayor and the Treasurers are now hereby to open the Treasury and to affix the Common Seal of this Corporation to an instrument of contract between this Corporation and William Chandler of this borough, a carpenter, for executing the work agreeably to the arrangement of the Committee for the sum of one thousand, three hundred and twenty pounds, payable at the respective times in the said instrument expressed. (29 August 1825) [3]

At the same Hall it was reported that the Schoolmaster had requested use of some land near the Greyfriars Tower, which was opposite the school house, as a garden:

The application of the Reverend John Bransby, Master of the Grammar School, requesting permission to convert part of the piece of land adjoining the Old Tower into a garden, being now read: Agreed that the said application be referred to the Land Committee, who are hereby authorised to grant the request, subject to an annual acknowledgement rent of two shillings and sixpence, for a limited term, and subject also to any other regulations which that Committee may think expedient. (29 August 1825) [4]

When the matter was debated by the Land Committee it was agreed that Mr Bransby should have the area next to the tower for a garden but it was decided that the annual rent should be ten shillings:

A request by the Master of the Grammar School for use of a piece of land adjoining the Tower as a garden was agreed at an annual rent of ten shillings to be paid on Michaelmas Day. He was to maintain a fence against the street and the remainder of the piece of land and was not to plant trees or shrubs against the theatre or the Old Tower. (26 September 1825) [5]

Note: The Old Tower referred to is the Greyfriars Tower and the theatre, previously the Theatre Royal, is now the Bingo Hall in St James Street.

In 1829 a request by the Schoolmaster to be granted relief from rates and taxes was not agreed but a year later the General Purposes Committee did sanction the painting of the house, both

Figure 20 The memorial stones on either side of the entrance to King Edward VII School

inside and out, at a cost not exceeding £20.

In 1829 and 1830 there are two interesting entries in the Hall Book concerning the award of the Titley Scholarship:

> A letter from Mr William Begley, (a scholar educated at this Grammar School), dated this day, praying for an Exhibition to Emmanuel College, being now read. Resolved that the Town Clerk be directed to refer to the original grant of the Exhibition in question and state his opinion to the next Hall whether it be obligatory on the Corporation to grant the same to every applicant without regard to his proficiency in classics or otherwise. (23 July 1829) [6]

The reference to proficiency in the classics is unclear but Mr Frederick Lane, then Deputy Town Clerk, did produce a very detailed report for the Corporation setting out the origins of the various scholarships and awards which he presented in August 1829. No further reference to the application by Mr Begley has been found in the Hall Book but according to Venn's *Alumni Cantabrigienses* [7] he 'migrated' from St John's College to Emmanuel in 1829 which would suggest that he was awarded the Titley Scholarship.

A further question relating to the award was raised the following year when Mr John Platten asked that the Titley Scholarship be awarded to his son Thomas, who had been a scholar at the Grammar School for five years when Mr Kidd was the Master and for about a year after Mr Bransby's arrival, but had then transferred to Wymondham to be under Mr Kidd again. Since he was not a scholar of the Grammar School when he completed his education his eligibility was in doubt. However the Corporation decided in his favour:

> The Mayor, Aldermen and Common Council do this day nominate and recommend Thomas Parlett Platten, late one of the scholars of the Grammar School of this borough, to one of the vacant Exhibitions or Scholarships, called Lynn Scholarship or Mr Titley's Scholarship in Emmanuel College in the University of Cambridge, with all the benefits, stipends and privileges appertaining to the said scholarships. (31 December 1830) [8]

The first sign of a dispute between John Bransby and the Corporation appears in 1833 and it concerned the right of Freemen to have their sons educated at the Grammar school free of charge. This long established custom had been reaffirmed in the 1747 Statutes as we saw in Chapter 5:

> Agreed that the Master of the Free Grammar School of this borough be directed to receive into that school the sons of all Freemen who shall be desirous of having their sons instructed in the Latin and Greek languages, and that the Town Clerk do give to the Master an official notification whenever any Freeman shall signify his desire for the instruction of his son into that school. (14 February 1833) [9]

By 1836 it was obvious that the Corporation was somewhat unhappy with the Schoolmaster but they needed to be sure that any action they might take would be according to custom and tradition:

> Ordered that the Town Clerk do lay before the Hall a return of the particulars of the endowment of the Grammar School and the salary and perquisites of the Master, and that the Master be requested to furnish the names of the scholars who had received instruction under the endowment during the last ten years. (22 January 1836) [10]

A report by the Town Clerk, dated 6 February 1836 [11] rehearsed the origins of the Grammar School and the possible links to Thomas Thoresby and a large number of entries relating to the school up to 1833 were reproduced from the Hall Books, along with details of the Titley, Hall, Peirson and Thurlin exhibitions:

Ordered that Report of the Town Clerk respecting the Grammar School be entered in the Book kept for similar entries with a view to more ready reference hereafter.

Agreed that the Report of the Town Clerk respecting the Grammar School be referred to the Mayor for the time being or his Deputy, Mr Robert Clifton, Mr Oxley English, Mr James Parlett Saddleton, Mr James Towell and Doctor Tweedale as a Committee to report thereupon and also all matters connected with the Grammar school with power for the Committee, or any three of them, to direct the Town Clerk to take the opinion of Counsel upon any point connected with the present reference. And the Committee are requested to make their report to this Hall as soon as they shall have maturely deliberated upon the subject. (10 February 1836) [12]

This special committee which met on the 25 February [13] was highly critical of the Schoolmaster in its report to the Council:

Your Committee regret to find that the Grammar School, which was instituted for the benefit of the rising generation, has failed to effect the result notwithstanding the liberal support it has received from the Corporation.

From the fact that only one application having been made during the last ten years for admission into the school (under the supposed foundation) it is evident that the funds appropriated to its support have been more than equal to the wants of the town for that kind of education. Your Committee cannot therefore by any means recommend any increase of expenditure, but consider it only an act of justice that some duty should be performed by the Master in return for his salary and for the use of the valuable premises which he occupies, for although the Master states that he was not bound by any agreement to educate any boys, yet he could not expect to hold the situation as a sinecure and evidently accepted the situation upon the same conditions as his predecessors. It appears to your Committee that the amount of salary has been increased from time to time and has entirely depended upon the free will of the Corporation and that the Corporation have an undoubted right to insist upon the education of a certain number of boys in proportion to the present amount of the Master's salary, and that such education should be adapted to the present wants of the town and not confined to Greek and Latin. Your Committee are of the opinion that a plain English education including Grammar, Penmanship and Arithmetic would in general be most useful, although the Master should be qualified to teach Greek and Latin and might be called upon so to do in particular cases.

Upon enquiry your Committee finds that boys are educated at other schools in the town for £4 4s a year; at that rate ten boys ought to be educated for the Master's salary of £40 a year and then there would be the annual value of the house and premises as a clear present to the Master, with permission to take other scholars.

Your Committee are of the opinion that the Master should be bound to educate from year to year any such ten boys as may be recommended by the Council either in English only or with the addition of the Classics as may appear most desirable to the Council.

Your Committee are of the opinion it would have been preferable if the salaries of the Master and Usher had been kept distinct and not paid to the Master in one sum as has been the case for several years past, because there has not always been an Usher employed and in some instances mere boys have been engaged in this service; and the last Usher having died there can be no occasion to engage another for the small number of boys now in the school. Should the Council ever deem it expedient to nominate more than ten boys your Committee recommend that four guineas a year should be paid by the Council for every boy so nominated, thus guarding against additional expense being incurred without any benefit received in return. Your Committee have no doubt but many well qualified gentlemen may be found (in case the present Master should decline these terms) to take the house and premises and educate the boys without any other advantages than that of [living] rent free.

Your Committee observes by the papers furnished them that an Usher was granted to a former Master in consequence of the Master's ill health* but that both the approval of the Usher and the payment of his salary rested entirely with the Corporation. The Master's appointment has always been during the pleasure of the Corporation.

Accompanying the report above was a recommendation that the Reverend John Bransby should be allowed to continue as Master if he would accept the new terms as set out but should otherwise be given notice as from the following midsummer, leaving him 'the enjoyment of such pension and allowance as he may be entitled to under the 68th section of the Municipal Corporation Act' (1835).

However when the report was submitted to a full meeting of the Council there was some disquiet about the proposals:

The Report of the Committee (dated 25 February 1836) respecting the Grammar School having been read:

Resolved that without adopting to the full extent of the language of the report wherein any inference can be drawn in relation to points where a difference of opinion may exist between individual members of the Council such report be received subject to the future determination of the Council with regard to its details.

Resolved also....that Mr Bransby be invited to attend this Council on Wednesday next with a view to a conference relative to the subject matter of the Grammar School. (10 March 1836) [14]

A week later the Council decided to ask the Town Clerk to continue his researches:

Resolved....that the Town Clerk be directed to search the Rolls Chapel and other Record Offices in London for the purpose of obtaining full evidence of the original Endowment of the Grammar School. (16 March 1836) [15]

As a result the Town Clerk prepared a further report for the Council which he presented on 9 May [16]. In this document Mr Lane goes over much of the ground on the history of the Grammar School found in his earlier report in February, but including some additional information and, in some respects, changes some of his earlier views. However he admits that he cannot present more definite conclusions. He expresses the hope that the Council will understand the problems involved in consulting documents of such antiquity and 'the extreme difficulty of deciphering writing as far back as the reign of Richard the Third, the necessity of translating many of the entries which appear in barbarous Latin and the impracticability of bestowing continuous application to the task in consequence of the strain upon the eyesight occasioned by fatiguing employment of this nature'. These reports are in fact impressive pieces of research.

However the Town Clerk's work was not yet finished for he was asked to take legal opinion both on the origins of the Grammar School and on the matters relating to the Master and the Usher which were of concern to the Corporation. He was also to let the Schoolmaster know that in the mean time he should make no further appointment of an Usher:

Town Clerk having laid before this assembly a further report relative to the Grammar School:

Ordered that the Town Clerk do proceed in the investigation and after having all the information within his reach touching the question of the Endowment that he do forthwith prepare a statement of case for the opinion of some eminent Chancery Counsel embracing all the points affecting the interests of the Corporation and the Master and Usher of the School and that he do lay the draft of

---

*22 December 1755

the case before the Committee already appointed to the Grammar School.

> Ordered also that the Town Clerk be directed to intimate to the Reverend John Bransby the wish of this Council that he make no fresh appointment of an Usher without the direction of the Council and to explain to him that it is probable that the salary of £23 will not be continued. (9 May 1836) [17]

In setting out the case for consideration by various eminent counsel the Town Clerk [18] stated that the view of the Corporation was that they were not responsible for the Grammar School, that the salary payments were merely voluntary and that the house could be appropriated to other purposes if they so wished. Further it was claimed that Thomas Thoresby's Trust became invalid after the Reformation and that the lands described in his will and subsequently granted to the Corporation by his son were 'their sole property unclothed with any trust for a grammar school.' The Town Clerk noted that the Schoolmaster on the other hand claimed that the school house could not be diverted from its present purpose and that he was entitled to the rents of the four pieces of pasture land at Gaywood that could be identified from Mr Thoresby's will.

The opinion of Edward Jacobs of Lincoln's Inn, dated 23 June 1836 [19], was that as the school house had been occupied by the Schoolmaster since the seventeenth century he felt that a Court of Equity would find that it had been effectively dedicated to that purpose. Under the 1835 Municipal Corporations' Act the Master was entitled to his salary of £40 per year, but not to the rents of any lands as well. He also expressed the view that the Corporation could dismiss the Master but if it did so he would still be entitled to his stipend. Neither did he think that the nature of the Master's duties could be changed without his consent.

In March 1837 it was decided that the allowance for the Usher would cease to be paid as from Lady Day (25 March):

> It was moved by Doctor Tweedale and seconded by Mr Towell that the Treasurer be directed to make no further payment to the Reverend John Bransby as a salary for the Usher of the Grammar School; but it was moved by Mr Alderman Cresswell and seconded by Mr Saddleton by way of amendment that the Treasurer be directed to pay the Reverend John Bransby the usual salary to the Usher of the Grammar School until Lady Day next but no longer and on a division the amendment was carried, the numbers being 15 in favour and 3 against it. (6 March 1837) [20]

Mr Bransby was keen to have the allowance for an Usher restored and contacted the Corporation on a number of occasions about the matter:

> The Town Clerk having laid before this assembly a letter from the Reverend John Bransby, Master of the Grammar School, urging his claim for a salary to the Usher,

> Agreed that the other business of the day be proceeded with. (9 November 1837) [21]

> The Reverend John Bransby, Master of the Grammar School, having addressed a letter to this Corporation requiring to be furnished with a sufficient bond or obligation for the payment of the salary and other allowances to which he was entitled or had been accustomed to receive for seven years before the operation of the recent act for the regulation of municipal corporations,

> Agreed that the application of Mr Bransby be referred to the Finance Committee together with the case and opinion of the Attorney General in relation to the Grammar School with the power for the Committee to direct the Town Clerk to make such additional statement for the further opinion of Counsel as the committee shall think advisable. (9 February 1838) [22]

In December 1837 the Attorney General, Sir John Campbell gave an opinion in which he stated that the under the Municipal Corporations' Amendment Act (1837) the Council retained the control and management of the Grammar School in King's Lynn and was obliged to continue the salaries of the Master and Usher even after the death of the incumbent. [23]

In addition Mr Flather of Lincoln's Inn expressed the opinion, dated 11 July 1839, [24] that the Master was entitled to the allowance for an Usher but also that he had to employ a suitable person. Further representations by Mr Bransby in 1840 were referred to the Finance Committee:

> The application of the Reverend John Bransby, Master of the Grammar School, for payment of arrears claimed by him in respect of the Usher's salary having been read,
>
> Agreed (Mr Bircham dissenting) that the subject be referred to the determination of the Finance Committee with the assistance of those members of the Council being of the legal profession as shall attend on summons after they shall have examined the cases and opinions of Counsel upon the subject and received proof from Mr Bransby that he actually has complied with the terms of his appointment by keeping an Usher. (9 May 1840) [25]

From 1833 a great deal of time and effort and money had been spent on this dispute with the Schoolmaster. However in October 1841 the General Purposes Committee recommended, albeit with great reluctance, that Mr Bransby should be paid the allowance for an Usher including arrears:

> The Town Clerk submitted the opinions of the late Attorney General, Sir John Campbell, and Mr Flather, that the Corporation did have an obligation to pay the Master of the Grammar School £23 per year for the Usher's salary, not withstanding the provisions of the Municipal Corporation Reform Act. It was agreed that Mr Bransby would be paid the arrears of the Usher's salary to Michaelmas last. The Committee recommended that for the future the Master of the Grammar School should be required to certify yearly to the Council before any further portion of the salary be paid that 'a good and sufficient Usher has been employed by him for the period for which he claims a future payment on account of the Usher's salary.' (28 October 1841) [26]

This recommendation was accepted by the Council on 9 November:

> Agreed that the report of the Committee for General Purposes on the twenty-eighth day of October last with reference to the Grammar School….be received and adopted by this Hall. (9 November 1841) [27]

By 1850 the Corporation was desperate to be rid of John Bransby but in the end had to offer him more money as a pension than he had been receiving in salary to finally achieve it:

> Resolved that in the opinion of the Committee no practical benefit can arise to the proper management of the Grammar School during the continuance of the Revd John Bransby as Master and the Committee unanimously determine to recommend to the Hall that Mr Bransby should be called upon to retire from the Mastership.
>
> Resolved also that a copy of the foregoing resolution be transmitted to the Revd John Bransby with an intimation that this Committee has adjourned until a future day to afford him an opportunity of conferring with the Committee prior to their final decision being submitted to the Hall. (2 November 1850) [28]

A letter from Mr Bransby had been received and he was also present for part of a meeting on 7 December. [29] He denied the power of the Council either to remove him or to interfere in the management of the school, but he was prepared 'to receive a proposal' from the Committee or the Hall. The Committee decided that to avoid the expense of legal proceedings it would recommend that he should be offered an annuity of £65 for life on his retiring from the

Mastership. This was communicated to Mr Bransby who declined to give an immediate reply. The Committee adjourned to Saturday 14 December when it was reported that Mr Bransby had agreed to resign as from Christmas if he was offered £70 a year for life. This was agreed. [30]

At the core of the dispute between the Corporation and the Schoolmaster were two matters of principle. The first concerned the right to a free education for the sons of Freemen, but the second was even more important and that was the increasing irrelevance in the nineteenth century of the traditional classical education. As early as February 1836 this view was strongly expressed at meetings of the Council. It is not surprising therefore that Mr Bransby's successor, the Reverend Francis Bagge Scott was employed under very different conditions of service, as we shall see in the next chapter.

8. Into the second half of the nineteenth century

Resolved unanimously that the Reverend Francis Bagge Scott, Master of Arts, late of Saint John's College in the University of Cambridge and now residing in Godmanchester in the County of Huntingdon be and he is hereby appointed Master of the Free Grammar School within this borough, on the resignation of the Reverend John Bransby, to hold the said Mastership from the twenty-fifth day of December last during the pleasure of the Mayor, Aldermen and Burgesses at the salary of forty pounds per annum, beside the use of the present dwelling house, school rooms, yards and appurtenances and with other accustomed privileges. And upon condition that the said Master do educate the sons of inhabitants or rated occupiers within the borough in the common course of Classics, Mathematics, Writing, Ciphering and the usual branches of English Literature at a sum not exceeding two guineas per quarter.

Agreed that the repairs to the Grammar School and premises attached thereto and which are enumerated in the estimate now delivered in be forthwith executed at an expense not exceeding two hundred and fifty pounds under the direction of the Grammar School Committee who are requested to superintend the same. (20 January 1851) [1]

So for the first time in three hundred years the Grammar School curriculum was broadened to take in subjects other than the Classical languages. This would inevitably increase the number of pupils ready to avail themselves of the education offered. The notion of a free education for the sons of freemen is not mentioned but a limit is set on the fees that can be charged to the sons of local inhabitants or rated occupiers. Soon after his arrival the Corporation agreed that the Schoolmaster should be paid the usual £23 a year to defray the expenses of employing an Usher and in 1853 the salary offered was considerably increased. This entry is also the first occasion on which the term Head Master is used:

A letter from the Reverend Francis Bagge Scott, Head Master of the Grammar School, intimating his intention to provide an Usher at a salary of seventy pounds per annum, one moiety of which he proposes to contribute himself and requesting that this Corporation will augment the present Usher's stipend from twenty-three pounds to thirty-five pounds per annum, to make the other moiety, having been read, agreed that the application be granted during pleasure. (31 March 1853) [2]

One of the concerns which came to the fore in Francis Bagge Scott's time as Head Master was the money available for the Grammar School Exhibitions to Cambridge and the conditions under which they should be granted:

The subject of the Exhibitions belonging to the Grammar School having been brought under the notice of this Hall by the Reverend Francis Bagge Scott, the present Master, agreed that no scholar from the above school shall be entitled to claim the Exhibitions unless he shall have been continuously educated therein for at least two years previously and proceed direct from the school to university. (22 September 1853) [3]

Two years later the Education Committee (7 November 1855) [4] considered the matter of accumulations of arrears. The Head Master had made representations to the Committee about arrears due for several of the Exhibitions belonging to the Grammar School still in the hands of the Corporation. The Town Clerk was asked to ascertain the amount of such arrears and order that an application be made to the Corporation for payment. Also it was recommended that the funds, relating to the several Exhibitions in the hands of the Corporation or the Charity Trustees and all future payments due, should be invested in the Savings Bank in the name of the Mayor, in order that the interest accumulate for the benefit of scholars going from the school to the

University of Cambridge.

The situation with regards to the various awards during this period is unclear. The Municipal Corporations Act of 1835 transferred the management of charitable funds which had been administered by the unreformed corporations to bodies of municipal charities. So for a period of about 50 years the Trustees of the King's Lynn Municipal Charities acted as custodians of the Titley, Peirson and Thurlin funds, but no records of any awards made by them have survived.

At the meeting of the Education Committee referred to above a problem arising from the payment of arrears to students who did not complete their university courses was discussed. A recent case had demonstrated that the benefits of the Exhibition had been lost because the gift and arrears had been paid to a scholar when he started at the university but he had left without completing his education. The Committee recommended that in future the money should be paid to the Tutor of the College to be spent in 'proper proportions during the period of the scholar's collegiate residence.'

Although this report was adopted at a full meeting of the Hall there are no further relevant entries until after the appointment of a new Head Master in 1858 following the death of the Reverend Bagge Scott. He had been ill for some time as shown by the following entry:

> Agreed that the thanks of this Hall be and the same are now hereby presented to Mr William J Hickie BA for the able and efficient manner in which he has discharged the duties connected with the Free Grammar School of this borough, during the absence occasioned by severe illness of the Reverend Francis Bagge Scott, Head Master of the said school, and that a copy of this minute be forwarded to Mr Hickie under the Corporate Seal. (9 November 1857) [5]

In August 1858 following the death of the Reverend Francis Bagge Scott the Head Mastership was advertised. The salary was substantially increased - from £40 to £75 per year - and there were additional sums available if the number of foundation scholars went above thirty. Interestingly the Corporation at this stage seemed to accept the link to the Thoresby benefaction since 1543 was the date of the indenture between Thomas Thoresby, the son, and the Lynn Corporation in which four pieces of pasture were transferred to the Mayor and Burgesses on condition that they appoint a Schoolmaster. The advertisement for the new Head Master was placed in *The Times* as well as in Oxford, Cambridge and Norfolk newspapers, and the detailed conditions of service, to be circulated to applicants, are printed below:

> Agreed that the following conditions, relating to the Headmastership of the school be adopted, printed, advertised and circulated:
>
> 1. The school was founded in the 35th Henry 8th [1543]. Patrons, the Council of the Borough.
>
> 2. The course of education is to comprise Classics, Mathematics, the French and German Languages, Elementary Science, English Literature, Arithmetic, Writing and Drawing and generally to embrace the class of subjects prescribed by the Middle Class examinations of the Universities, the examinations of the Society of Arts and the competitive examinations of the Government.
>
> 3. The Master will be bound to educate the sons of inhabitants of the Borough in the above course at not more than five guineas per half year.
>
> 4. The Master will be entitled to receive and educate pupils not included in the above limitation upon his own terms.
>
> 5. Attached to the school are several Exhibitions to the University of Cambridge, namely two to

Emmanuel College, one to Saint John's, one to Trinity and one to any college in the University and as these Exhibitions have not been claimed for many years there are considerable accumulations of the several funds.

6. All pupils, as well boarders as foundation scholars, will be eligible as Exhibitioners.

7. The minimum salary payable to the Master will be £75, to be increased by ten guineas for every five foundation pupils above 30, until it reaches 100 guineas.

8. The Master will be entitled to the free occupation of the house, school rooms and playground attached. The house comprises dining hall and bedroom accommodation for 60 or 70 boarders, exclusive of private rooms for the use of a family.

9. The appointment of the Master will be quamdiu se bene gesserit [as long as he shall behave himself well], and the duties of the office will commence on 11th day of October next. It is a condition of the appointment that the Master should be experienced in tuition.

Guild Hall, King's Lynn 11th August 1858. [6]

The advertisement attracted a field of some 35 applicants, four of who were called for interview:

The proceedings of the meeting of the Council held on the fifth day of August last having been read over, and the letters and testimonials of the candidates for the Head Mastership of the Grammar School of the town having been perused and fully considered, the Council agreed to select the Reverend Horatio Ward (Westbourne Park, London), the Reverend H M Crowther (King's Bridge, Devon), the Reverend Thomas White (Loughborough) and the Reverend J Montague (Warwick) as being most eminently qualified and, resolved that the further consideration of the selected testimonials should be adjourned until Wednesday the twenty-second instant at 11 am for the purpose of election, and that the above selected candidates be apprised of this intention and be invited to attend such meeting with their original testimonials, and that in the meantime their testimonials do lie at the office of the Town Clerk for the further perusal of members of this Hall. Ordered that the testimonials of the unselected candidates be forthwith returned to them. (8 September 1858) [7]

Much greater weight seems to have been placed on the value of open testimonials than would be the case today. At the meeting held on 22 September the Reverend Thomas White was selected and he remained as Head Master until 1874. He had been a student at St John's College, Cambridge, graduating in 1852 and receiving his MA in 1855. In 1871 he was awarded the degree of Doctor of Law. Before taking up the appointment in Lynn he had been Second Master at Loughborough School for six years.

Very soon after his appointment he took up the matter of the Grammar School Exhibitions with the Mayor and Burgesses. He attended a meeting of the Education Committee on 26 November 1858 [8] and made the following recommendations concerning the eligibility of applicants for the various awards:

1. They be in the gift of the Mayor and Corporation on the recommendation of the Head Master.

2. No boy would be recommended unless he had attended the Grammar School for two complete consecutive years at least before leaving for the university and in the opinion of the Head Master was likely to distinguish himself at the university.

3. The Exhibitions to be tenable for three years.

4. The value of each Exhibition to be decided.

5. Each Exhibition to be paid yearly in three equal instalments – at the start of each university term.

6. Each Exhibition to be held only during good behaviour and continued residence at the college.

Although these recommendations were accepted by the Education Committee at their meeting on 11 March 1859 and recommended to the Corporation no final decision was made at the next full Meeting:

> The Report of the Educational Committee respecting the Grammar School dated the eleventh day of March last having been read, agreed that the recommendation there contained as to the application of the Exhibitions belonging to the school be referred back to the Committee, with a request that they will obtain a statement showing the fund now in hand belonging to the Exhibitions, and report thereon to a future Hall. (21 April 1859) [9]

The Town Clerk produced the requested information for the Education Committee at its meeting on 19 November 1859:

Emmanuel College:	Amount in hand - £182 at Lady Day 1859
Peirson's Exhibition:	Amount in hand - £49 at Lady Day 1859
Dr Thurlyn's Exhibition:	Amount in hand - £132 at Lady Day 1859
Dr Hopes's Exhibition:	Amount in hand - £37 15s 4d in 1854

At the same meeting it was:

> Agreed on the recommendation of the Head Master that it be submitted to the Hall to grant the sum of £30 per annum out of Thurlyn's Exhibition Fund to Thomas Oldmeadow Price; also £15 per annum from Peirson's Exhibition to Alfred Legge, each for three years.

> Agreed that it be recommended to the Hall to cause application to be made to the Charity Commissioners for an order to consolidate all the Exhibitions belonging to the Grammar School, accompanied with a direction that the same be thrown open to any of the universities of the kingdom. [10]

However no ratification of the latter recommendation has been found in the Hall Books and this matter was not settled until the 1880s.

In 1863 a letter from Mr White asked for help on behalf of Walter Begley of King's Lynn and Charles Eller of West Winch who were students at Corpus Christi College and Queens' College respectively. His suggestion was that they should be given grants from the accumulations in the Titley funds, arguing that 'the University Commission has in a vast number of cases abolished restrictions attached to similar endowments; and in dispensing with one of the provisions of the founder for the special case the Council will be following a very respectable precedent.' He also suggested that Mr Begley, as a native of Lynn could be awarded the Peirson and Hall Exhibitions.

> Resolved unanimously….that a formal application be made to the Charity Commissioners to sanction the proposed appropriation. (30 November 1863) [11]

Mr White had clearly got the bit between his teeth because in a further letter to the Corporation he asked about the payment of arrears in respect of Hall's Exhibition. Having taken legal advice, the Town Clerk reported in May 1864 that scholars were not entitled to any arrears.

It was not without considerable time and effort that Mr Begley received the £2 per year claimed. An entry in the Hall Book records the notice given to the owner of the property on the site of Hall's warehouse and a response from her solicitor in London:

> The Town Clerk having reported that at the request of the Master of the Grammar School, he had given a notice signed by Walter Begley, a native of Lynn, and now a scholar at the University of

Cambridge, requesting payment of the annual sum of forty shillings payable under the will dated the 27th day of July 1597 of Alexander Hall to a poor scholar born in Lynn, going from there to the University of Cambridge, by delivering such notice at the residence of Mrs Catherine Southwell, the owner of the property alleged to be charged by the said will with the payment of the said sum, and that he had been in personal communication with her son-in-law therein, and the following letter from Mr E Williamson of Red Lion Square, London, her solicitor having been read ….(2 January 1865) [12]

After other letters to and from the Charity Commissioners the matter was finally settled in August 1865:

And it was ordered that the Town Clerk be instructed to call the attention of the Paving Commission to the fact that they have purchased the property in New Conduit Street chargeable with the payment of Hall's Exhibition and to suggest that they will provide for the Exhibition when payable. (2 August 1865) [13]

Among Mr White's greatest successes as Head Master was undoubtedly securing the patronage of the Prince of Wales in 1864 with the award of a Gold Medal for the best student at the Grammar School, a prize which is awarded annually to this day:

Read a letter sent to the Mayor by the Reverend Thomas White, the Head Master of the Grammar School, intimating the intention of His Royal Highness the Prince of Wales to offer yearly a Gold Medal for competition in the school.

Resolved unanimously….that the cordial thanks of the Council be expressed to His Royal Highness for the handsome and appropriate form in which His Highness has testified his interest in the prosperity of the school. (1 January 1864) [14]

It is believed that the Grammar School was brought to the attention of the Prince of Wales when the boys lined the station at Lynn to welcome the newly married royal couple on their way to Sandringham, which had been bought for the Prince of Wales as a private house in 1862. The first medal was awarded to H Bristow in April 1865 and since then it has been awarded every year with the exception of two years in the late 1880s when the school was in a poor state. The 1880/81 Gold Medal, awarded to George Mossop, is shown in Figure 21. It was returned to King

Figure 21 The Royal Gold Medal for 1880/81 awarded to George Mossop

Edward VII School in 1945 but unfortunately was stolen along with many silver cups in 1980.

Mr White was very successful and the school thrived during his time as Head Master. However there was one disagreement with the Council and it was again about the provision of free education:

> It was….agreed that it be referred to the Educational Committee to take into consideration the circumstances attending the exclusion of the free boys from the Grammar School and that they be requested to report thereon, and also as to the terms upon which the Reverend Thomas White accepted the Headmastership of the school. (9 February 1865) [15]

However the Head Master was able to show that the terms on which he was employed made no mention of free boys and the Education Committee came to the conclusion that there was nothing to be done:

> Your Committee have met to consider the matters referred to them, and they are of the opinion that as regards the Headmastership it is not open to the Corporation to make any alteration in the terms of admission to the school, as long as the present Headmaster retains his appointment. (26 April 1865) [16]

In fact in advertisements for the school, Mr White not only boasted of 'the unusual distinction of a valuable Gold medal, given annually as a Prize by HRH the Prince of Wales and presented by His Royal Highness in person at Sandringham House' but also of the fact that there were 'no free boys'.

In 1865 the Royal Schools' Inquiry Commission requested information on the origins and current state of the Lynn Grammar School and both the Education Committee and Mr White responded. The latter in a twenty-two page statement rehearses the origins of the school and concludes that it was doubtful whether Thomas Thoresby's bequest could be considered as the endowment of the school which he says was in existence before Thoresby's time. He argues that John Baxter [Rackster] was re-appointed in 1550 on new conditions. However no evidence was provided for these assertions. White's view on the matter was coloured by the fact that he was against the education of free boys at the Grammar School which he said would be an anachronism and would speedily drive away all but free boys. 'The loss to the town in such a case would far outweigh the benefits of such a questionable charity to a few individuals.' He also argues, again from a not unbiased point of view, 'that the town receives a full and adequate equivalent for the emoluments it confers on the Master'. [17]

We rarely have information on the numbers of the scholars at the Grammar School but the average number of boys over the previous six years was contained in the information supplied by Mr White to the Schools' Inquiry Commission in February 1865:

	Day Boys	Boarders
Boys under 10 years of age	3	1
Boys aged 10-14	19	9
Boys over 14 years of age	8	10
Totals	30	20

Mr J L Hammond MA, the Assistant Commissioner for Norfolk (and Northumberland) reported:

> The school is attended by about 45 boys, of whom nearly 20 are boarders (AD 1865). The number of day boys approaches but, under the present master, has never exceeded 30. They are chiefly the sons of professional men, farmers and respectable tradespeople. All learn Latin. French, history,

geography, English grammar and English Literature are professedly taught throughout the school. About half the boys learn Greek, German, mathematics and drawing. The school thus attempts to provide a certain amount of preparation for the universities with a good general education of a more practical character. [18]

He says that it was in the latter respect that it was most successful. However he then goes on to refer to various distinctions gained by the scholars in competitive or university local examinations. In general he was complimentary about the Lynn Grammar School. He was particularly impressed by the teaching of arithmetic, which he said was much better in Norfolk than Northumberland, and that 'the papers from the King's Lynn Grammar School were excellent.' He went on to say that 'English and other subjects in which the school enters more directly into competition with private commercial academies are on the whole as successfully taught as in the best of them.'

In May 1865 Mr White requested the help of the Corporation to hold a Cambridge Local Examination in Lynn:

An application by the Reverend Thomas White, the Head Master of the Grammar School, that the Corporation should empower the Educational Committee or any select number of themselves to act with him as the Committee for managing a Cambridge Middle Class Local Examination to be held in Lynn next December and that the Committee should be authorised to defray one half the expense or about five pounds. It was moved….that his request be complied with provided that the number of candidates for the examination be not less than fifteen, and that the expense to be born by the Corporation shall not exceed five pounds. (10 May 1865) [19]

In these examinations nine boys were successful, one at honours standard, and were awarded certificates, which the Head Master described as being much more valuable than testimonials, as well as being accepted by the legal and medical professions as a substitute for their own preliminary professional examinations. [20]

We have more information than in previous times about the Grammar School during Thomas White's time as Head Master because the School Archive contains a book which records the curriculum taught, samples of work by students such as Thomas Oldmeadow Price, Alfred Legge and Walter Begley, along with reports of the annual Speech days for the years 1865-74. In 1867, for example, there were six assistant masters, including Sergeant Lorimer of the 54th Foot who taught drill. There was a Second Master, a French and German Master, a Music Master, a lecturer on Physics and an English and Commercial Master. There were special external examiners for the Gold Medal and for mathematics. The latter was former student, Walter Begley BA, of Corpus Christi, College, Cambridge.

We also have some accounts of the School at the time Dr White was Headmaster, albeit written at a much later date, which may explain some of the discrepancies, for example in the way the school room was heated. G G Coulton (1867-71) and R C Hitchcock (1871-76) have both described the very poor physical environment in which they had to learn:

The school itself was situated in an ordinary house in St James' Street, facing the theatre and the 'Old Tower'. A narrow passage from the street door led to the playground behind, gravelled and about sixty feet square. This was squeezed in among other houses; but its eastern side was mainly taken up by the schoolroom, a sort of shed perhaps forty feet long. Inside, it was furnished with two desks at the south-east and south-west corners, for the Head and Second Masters, and a third at the north-east for the usher or Modern Language Master. I do not think there were ever more than three teaching there at the same time; sometimes, indeed, there were only two; for the Head was often taking a class in his own dining room which overlooked the street....The room was heated by a single iron stove at the end of the two senior desks, while draughts poured in from the ill-fitting door and windows. Much of our work was done on slates: these we cleaned with spittle, and then claimed the right of drying them at the stove. [21]

Imagine a big room, with a door in the middle of one of the longer sides, windows on the west side looking into the yard, but those towards the east high up in the walls, with a good view of the chimney pots of neighbouring houses, a wide fireplace at each end of the room, thronged by boys in the intervals in the endeavour to get warm. The classes were held in each corner, none of them at first screened off in any way, but later screens were erected round two of the corners, where the Head and another Master did their work. The centre of the room was filled with desks, usually occupied by classes preparing work. Sometimes the Head would take a form in his house. There was a staff of three Masters in addition to the Head, a second Master who taught Classics, a French Master, and a Junior Form Master, who took English subjects. I cannot recall any Science subjects were taken in the School....Sport did not find a large place in the school life at that time. The School playing field was somewhere in the direction of the Chase, a long walk from the School, and I don't think many Day Boys made much use of it excepting on certain special half holidays when a visit to the field was made compulsory. [22]

In 1874 Dr White (LLD 1871) accepted the living of Hambledon in Hampshire. In his resignation letter he tries to ensure that his successor has no changes to the terms and conditions of the appointment imposed upon him:

Read the following communication from the Revd Dr White, the Head Master of the King's Lynn Grammar School, announcing his intended resignation, in the following terms (that is to say):

To the Mayor and Burgesses of King's Lynn

Worshipful Sir and Gentlemen

Having accepted preferment in the church, I have to inform you of my intended resignation of the Head Mastership of this school at Michaelmas next, and in giving back to your hands the trust you confided in me many years ago, I have great satisfaction in being able to thank you most cordially for the uniform support and courtesy which I have received from you all. It will be with reluctance that I quit the scene of my labours during the most important period of my life, and I trust that I may find in my new home as much friendliness as I have be so fortunate as to enjoy in this town. I am willing to retain the responsibility of the school until Michaelmas but it is most desirable that you should lose no time in selecting my successor. The school is at present in a flourishing condition, but long delay in announcing the appointment of a new Master will tend to scatter the boarders and it would take time to fill the school again.

I should like also to suggest, in the interest of the school, which must also be the interest of the Borough, that little or no change be made to the regulations for the government of the school; they have worked extremely well during my tenure of office and I cannot suggest any improvement in them.

I shall be happy to do all in my power to assist you in transferring to other hands the administration of this ancient Grammar School.

Believe me Gentlemen
Your humble and obliged servant
Thomas White

PS. In case your choice of my successor is made in time I should be desirous, with your permission, of arranging with him to commence his duties at the beginning of the term. (13 July 1874) [23]

When the Council discussed the appointment the following recommendations were made:

Grammar School Headmastership. Report of Committee.

Read the recommendation of the Committee of the Whole Hall in reference to the terms and conditions to be adopted on the appointment of a Head Master of the Grammar School in the place of the Revd Dr White, about to resign, that is to say:

1. The school is an ancient foundation. The Patrons are the Mayor, Aldermen and Burgesses.

2. The course of education is to comprise Classics, Mathematics, the French and German Languages, Elementary Science, English Literature, Arithmetic, Writing and Drawing.

3. The Master will be bound to educate the sons of the inhabitants of the Borough, who shall be considered Foundationers, in the above course, on the following terms viz:

    If under 10 years at the rate of 6 guineas a year

    If under 12 years at the rate of 8 guineas a year

    If over 12 years at the rate of 10 guineas a year

4. The Master will be entitled to receive and educate pupils not included in the above limitations upon his own terms.

5. Attached to the school are several Exhibitions to the University of Cambridge viz. two to Emmanuel College, one to Saint John's, one to Trinity and one to any other college in the University, but they are considered to be subject to any alterations that may hereafter be made.

6. The salary payable to the Head Master will be at the rate of £75 a year.

7. The Head Master will also be entitled to the free occupation of the school house, playground and school rooms attached; the house comprises dining hall and bedroom accommodation for about forty boarders, exclusive of private rooms for the use of a family.

8. The appointment of the Master will be quamdiu se bene gesserit [as long as he shall behave himself well], and the duties of the office will commence on the 11th of October next, or earlier by arrangement with the retiring Head Master.

9. The Master must be in Holy Orders and a Master of Arts at least, of the University of Oxford or Cambridge, and must have graduated in Honours at one of these universities. He must also be married and experienced in tuition.

An amendment to admit 4 boys from other schools in Lynn by competitive examination was not carried. However another amendment was agreed unanimously:

That in future any ordinary internal repairs that may be required to be done to the school house and school buildings, be done by the Master.

It was also agreed, that in addition to the paper recommended by the Committee, the vacancy be advertised in a Cambridge and in an Oxford paper, and that the applications be sent to the Mayor on or before Wednesday the 12th instead of the 5th of August next. (22 July 1874) [24]

The decision to make the Head Master pay for internal repairs and decorations was a major departure from tradition but perhaps had been prompted by the regular sums of money spent on the school during Dr White's tenure.

Dr White's successor, the Reverend John Bullivant Slight (1874 to 1887), was the last Head Master to be appointed by the Corporation, since a new Instrument of Government would be introduced in 1884. In contrast to the previous occasion in 1858 there were only six applicants for the post, two of whom were interviewed. John Slight (Figure 22) was appointed on the terms set out above although he did manage to get some repairs and decorations carried out before the new rules were applied:

> The Borough Treasurer also reported that the Reverend J B Slight, the Master of the Grammar School, had applied to have the interior of the school house and school room repainted, papered and coloured, the ceilings repaired and the school room windows made to open. And it is ordered that the application be referred to the Property Committee with power to act. (22 October 1874) [25]

The Property Committee (6 November 1874) took into consideration the question of the repairs to the interior of the Grammar School premises, referred to them at the last Hall, and these were agreed. However it was noted that in future the Head Master would be responsible for repairs to the interior and would be expected to leave it in a proper state of repair 'at the determination of his office'. [26]

Mr Slight was soon to discover he would have to bear the additional cost of repairs:

> The Surveyor reported that he had received an application from the Reverend J B Slight, Head Master of the Grammar School, asking for the repair of the brick floor in the lavatory, and of the sink stone in the scullery, and that he estimated the cost at £3 15s. And it is agreed that as Mr Slight had undertaken, under his agreement with the Corporation, to do all interior repairs to the school premises, the application cannot be entertained. (9 October 1876) [27]

> Read a letter from the Reverend J B Slight, asking for reconsideration by the Hall of his application, through the Borough Surveyor, for some repairs to be done to the Grammar School house, and stating that the repairs in question are substantial repairs of the fabric, and are made necessary by the wear and tear that took place before his time....The application was not acceded to. (9 November 1876) [28]

The matter of repairs and developments became a continuing theme during the next few years and Mr Slight was usually only successful in getting work done to the exterior of the property, although some work agreed in 1880 proved to be the exception:

> Read a letter from the Reverend J B Slight, the Master of the Grammar School, stating that he was anxious to be build two permanent rooms, one to be used as a carpenter's shop, and the other as a fives court, at the Grammar School, at an estimated cost of £155, and asking for help towards it from the Hall. And it was agreed that this Hall regrets it cannot assist in the matter. (9 February 1877) [29]

> Ordered that the exterior of the Grammar School house and premises be painted, the work to be done by tender, and under the direction of the Borough Treasurer. (20 June 1877) [30]

> Read an application from the Reverend J B Slight, the Head Master of the Grammar School, with reference to certain repairs required to the school

Figure 22 The Reverend J B Slight, Head Master 1874 to 1887

premises and grounds. And it is ordered that the matter be referred to the Property Committee to report to the Hall thereon. (9 February 1880) [31]

Read the Minutes of the proceedings of the same day [16 February] of the same Committee [Property] as to the application of the Master of the Grammar School for repairs as under, to be done for the school premises viz.

The floor of the kitchen to be re-laid
The lavatory floor to be re-laid in part
Fresh gravel in the school playground

And their report that numbers 1 and 2 ought to be done by the Corporation and number 3 by the Master. And it is ordered that their report be approved of and adopted, and as regards numbers 1 and 2, the work be done by the Corporation. (17 March 1880) [32]

The next few years saw much discussion on the future of the Grammar School. The Charity Commission in a letter to the Corporation in March 1881 stated that it was their intention to prepare a scheme for the administration of the school under the Endowed Schools' Act of 1869. A number of meetings took place between the two parties and various objections to the initial draft scheme were made by the Corporation. Eventually in December 1883 the final scheme was agreed:

Ordered that the Common Seal be affixed to the consent in writing now laid before the Hall, to the arrangement embodied in the first clause of the Draft Scheme of the Charity Commission for the Grammar school and Exhibition of Titley and others, and for the payment by the Corporation of the annual sum of £88 8s 4d for the purposes of the school. (19 December 1883) [33]

The sum of £88 8s 4d to be paid to the Grammar School annually by the Corporation was arrived at by adding to the salary of the Head Master (£75) the average cost of external repairs over the previous 15 years which was calculated to be £13 8s 4d. This sum of £88 8s 4d, together with a further £21 from 1910, the value of the Exhibitions arising from the wills of John and Mary Titley (1585 and 1595), Alexander Hall (1597), John Peirson (1623) and Thomas Thulin (1708), was paid by the King's Lynn Corporation (and its successor after 1974) up to 1998 when £3000 was accepted by the Governors of King Edward Vll School in lieu of any further payments.

The 1884 Instrument of Government for the Grammar School made provision for seven representative governors, nominated by HRH The Prince of Wales, the King's Lynn Town Council (2), the Trustees of the Municipal Charities, and three Cambridge Colleges, Trinity, St John's and Emmanuel. The Mayor was to be an ex-officio governor and there were to be in addition four co-optative governors:

Read an Order in Council of the 9th day of September last confirming the Scheme of the Charity Commissioners for England and Wales relative to the King's Lynn Grammar School and Titley Exhibition, whereby it provided amongst other things that two Representative Governors shall be appointed by the Town Council of King's Lynn. And it is agreed that Alderman J O Smetham and Councillor George Holditch be appointed to be Representative Governors of the King's Lynn Grammar School on behalf of the Town Council. (10 November 1884) [34]

From 1884 the main entries in the Hall Books and Committee Books concern the school exhibition funds and the proposal by William Lancaster to build a new school, more of which will be said in the final chapter.

9. Under new management

One of the clauses in the 1884 Instrument of Government made provision for the award of an Exhibition which was to be called the Titley Exhibition. The various funds were to be combined to provide a grant of £25 a year tenable for three years at any college in the University of Cambridge. Hence the school's new Governing Body when it took over in 1884 was keen to gain control of the exhibition funds and at the beginning of 1885 a small sub-committee was set up to enquire into the state of the accounts. It was discovered that the payments for the Titley, Thurlin and Peirson awards were made by the Corporation, half yearly, to the Trustees of the Municipal Charities. The money for the Titley Exhibition was paid by the Trustees to Emmanuel College, while the other two accumulated in the hands of the Trustees when not used. There were accumulations in each of the funds:

Titley's Exhibition:	£ 100	00s	0d
Thurlin's Exhibition:	£ 14	18s	4d
Peirson's Exhibition:	£ 5	4s	1d
Hopes' Exhibition:	£ 26	13s	1d (held by Trinity College)
Hall's Exhibition:	no accumulations		

The Governors decided to ask for the accumulated funds and requested that the annual payments be made directly to them in future. It took until 1888 for all the parties to reach agreement, although the accumulation funds held by Emmanuel College and Trinity College were paid to the School within months of the request being made.

> Read a letter from the Secretary to the Governors of the Grammar School applying for payment of the monies due to the Governors under the Grammar School Scheme and asking that the Corporation will if possible pay to the Governors all the monies usually paid to the Charity Trustees in respect of the School Exhibition after the payments to be made to the Charity Trustees in April 1885 and further inviting the attention of the Corporation to Hall's Exhibition. Read also an application from Mr W Hitchcock applying for payment of Hall's Exhibition for 4 years to his son, who is at the University of Cambridge, which has not been paid for some years. And it was agreed that the subjects of the letters be referred to the Rights Committee for consideration generally and to report thereon, and with power to put themselves in communication with the Municipal Charity Trustees in the matter. (18 March 1885) [1]

In May 1885 the Corporation agreed to pay Hall's Exhibition to Earnest Edward Hitchcock for the years 1882, 1883 and 1884 and at the same meeting agreed to a similar award to William Hunter Bennell for the years 1879, 1880 and 1881:

> Read the Minutes of the proceedings of the 27th March last of the Rights Committee in reference to the Grammar School Exhibition and their recommendations as to the payments in future being, with the assent of the Charity Trustees, made direct to the Grammar School Governors, and as to the payment of Hall's Exhibition for 1882, 1883 and 1884 to Ernest Edward Hitchcock. And it is ordered that the same be adopted and that payment be made to Ernest Edward Hitchcock accordingly.

> Read a letter of the 8th April 1885 from Mr W H Bennell stating that he had been informed that during his residence at Cambridge as an undergraduate from October 1878 to January 1882, he was entitled, as a native of Lynn and a pupil of the Grammar school, to Hall's Exhibition of £2 a year and, that not being aware thereof, he had omitted to claim same, and applying for a payment of the amount. And it is ordered that it be paid to him for the years 1879, 1880 and 1881. (11 May 1885) [2]

Partly as a result of the need to consult the Charity Commissioners it took another three years before there was a decision by the Corporation to pay the monies for the awards to the Lynn Grammar School Governors:

> Read a letter of the 17th January last from the Charity Commission stating that the Trustees of the Municipal Charities having ceased to be Trustees of the Grammar School and a separate Governing Body having been appointed for its management, it is open to the Corporation to pay Titley's, Pierson's and Thurlyn's Exhibitions of £11, £2 and £6 respectively direct to the Governors of the Grammar School instead of through the Charity Trustees and that it will be satisfactory to the Charity Commission to hear that the same will be done in future. And it was resolved…. that the same be in future paid direct to the Governors of the school. (21 March 1888) [3]

The first award was made by the Governors in 1885 to W J Swann who received a grant of £40 from the accumulated funds returned by Emmanuel and Trinity Colleges. Then in October 1886 Arthur T Tallent was awarded the first Titley Exhibition of £25 per year for three years. The second Titley Exhibitioner was Hamilton Drawbridge from 1889.

The regulations were further modified by the 1903 and 1910 Instruments of Government. The first specified that a sum of £21 per year was to be paid to the School by the Corporation arising from the wills of Thomas and Elizabeth Titley (£11), Thomas Thurlyn (£6), Alexander Hall (£2) and John Pierson (£2). The 1910 Scheme also stated that a payment of £3 8s 8d for the Hopes's Scholarship was to be paid to the School by the Rector of North Runcton.

Some information about the Grammar School under the Reverend J B Slight is contained in the Log Book begun by his predecessor, Dr White, although the entries continue for only one year and no further book has been found. However in the Governors' Minutes (21st October 1886) [4] are reports from the Head Master and the School Examiners, the Revd H J Sharpe MA and E J Rapson MA. The examiners were complimentary about the standard of work both by individual boys and in general. Mr Sharpe, for example, was pleased with Arthur Tallent's work in Mathematics: 'It shows honest, hard steady labour and promise all round'. In more general terms he said that 'the school maintains its excellent record in this most important subject' [arithmetic]. In commenting on the work in Classics and English, Mr Rapson concluded 'that in Lynn Grammar School a high degree of excellence in each has been attained.' He also said, 'The divinity paper was excellently done, and I can scarcely speak too highly of the thoughtfulness and care which mark the answers of several members of the sixth and upper fifth forms.'

In the same minutes the Head Master was reported to have expressed his satisfaction on the general health of the school, the discipline and standards of achievement, as shown by the examiners' reports and by the successes in the Cambridge Examinations. However he was worried about the fall in numbers, especially of boarders. Whether this was a factor in bringing about his downfall is unclear but in 1887 he was declared bankrupt and his resignation as Head Master was inevitable:

> It was resolved that in accordance with clause (27) of the Scheme, that the Revd J B Slight be dismissed from the office of Head Master of the King's Lynn Grammar School and that six month's calendar notice be given him in writing of such resolution. (Special Meeting of the Governing Body held at the Guild Hall on 20th April 1887) [5]

In fact this dismissal would not have been valid since the Scheme required a resolution to be passed at two special meetings at an interval of not less than 14 days and passed by not less than two thirds of the governors present. In the event Mr Slight offered his resignation:

> The Revd J B Slight's letter of 25 April 1887 resigning the post of Head Mastership to the King's

Lynn Grammar School having been read, his resignation was accepted by the Governing Body and the Chairman was requested to notify the same to the Revd J B Slight. (11 May 1887) [6]

At the same meeting a motion concerning a sale of furniture belonging to the Headmaster was passed unanimously:

> That the Governors understand with regret that it is proposed that a sale of the furniture belonging to the Head Master shall be held immediately. The permanent interests of the School would in the opinion of the Governors have suffered much less detriment if this sale could have been postponed till the vacation....The Chairman was requested to forward the same to the Trustees of assignment.[6]

The matter of the furniture was again raised at a meeting on 23 May:

> The question of purchasing the school furniture belonging to the Head Master having been considered, it was agreed that it was not incumbent upon the Governors to incur the responsibility of adopting such a course, more especially by reason of the fact of the Head Master having already returned the boarders to their respective homes. [7]

An advertisement for a replacement for Mr Slight was agreed by the Governors at the meeting on 23 May but the saga of Mr Slight's unfortunate position continued in June with not much sympathy being shown:

> A bill amounting to £11 14s for the board and lodging of the Assistant Masters at the Temperance Hotel since the bankruptcy of the Head Master was considered and it was agreed that the bill be referred to the Head Master for payment and in the event of his declining to pay the same that it be paid by the Governors and deducted from the next payment to him.

> Read a letter from Mr Hurlimann stating that the Head Master can no longer maintain him and asking the Governing Body to provide him with board and lodging. And it was agreed that the letter be referred to the Head Master, it being a private arrangement between Mr Hurlimann and the Head Master. (7 June 1887) [8]

At the end of the month a temporary arrangement whereby Mr Slight would carry on until the end of term was agreed:

> Read a letter from the Revd J B Slight asking the Governors to make an allowance to carry on the School until the end of the term at the rate of £4 per week from 25th May, the date of the sale, and for back payments in respect of his salary. And it was agreed that if Mr Slight will carry on the School till the end of term the Governors will advance him £3 per week from 2 July next as a temporary managing Master, to be deducted from money due to him from the Governors at the expiration of his office as Head Master. (Minutes, 28 June 1887) [9]

Not surprisingly in the circumstances the Governors declined to give Mr Slight a testimonial:

> It was stated by the Chairman that a request had been made to him by Mr Slight, the late Head Master, for a testimonial upon his leaving the School. And it was unanimously agreed that whilst wishing Mr Slight success in his future life the Governing Body is not called upon under the circumstances in giving a testimonial to him. (11 July 1887) [10]

When Mr Slight applied for the post in 1874 he had supplied no fewer than 16 testimonials, including one from his predecessor Dr White who had taught him at Loughborough. Fortunately the former Head Master of Brighton College, where Mr Slight had worked before coming to King's Lynn, was Vicar at Sandridge in Hertfordshire and offered him the post of Curate. He stayed there until 1891 when he became Rector at Moreton in Essex, a post he held until 1919. When Mr Slight died in 1928 his funeral was held at Moreton with no fewer than five priests officiating and a large number of his former parishioners present. He was clearly held in very high esteem in later life and as the photograph (Figure 23) suggests his fortunes had been considerably restored.

The next Head Master of the Lynn Grammar School was the Reverend Walter Boyce (1887 to 1919). He was to make the school more successful than it had ever been in its long history and to preside over the very important move from the old school in St James Street to the magnificent new building designed by Basil Champneys on the Gaywood Road. He was appointed from a field of 49 candidates in July 1887, having been Assistant Master at Ipswich School. Figure 24 shows Mr Boyce wearing the insignia of the Royal Victorian Order.

One relevant entry in the Hall Book concerns the use of the garden next to the Greyfriars Tower first granted to the Reverend John Bransby for his use in 1825:

> Read a letter from the Revd Walter Boyce, the Head Master of the Grammar School, asking to be allowed the same privileges as his predecessor as regards the occupation of the garden opposite the school house, and the privilege of cricket playing in a field belonging to the Corporation. And it is agreed that he be permitted to occupy the garden upon a payment of £4 a year rent for it, subject to this that the door to the Theatre is not to be blocked up in any way, but with respect to providing a playing field for the Grammar School pupils no action be taken. It is also agreed that the Headmaster is to have the charge of the key of the Greyfriars Tower during the pleasure of the Mayor for the time being. (28 September 1887) [11]

Mr Boyce was a very keen sportsman and wanted to gain access to a field for games for the boys at the Grammar School. The Governors' Minutes show that he rented a field for cricket and football from summer 1888, initially at £5 per term. The next reference in the Corporation records after that printed above is from 1898 but clearly Mr Boyce had been renting a field before that time as indicated in the following minute of the Property Committee:

> Read also an application from the Revd W Boyce for the use of the (Walks) Field for football and cricket for the Grammar School on weekdays other than Saturdays and otherwise upon the same terms as he has hitherto held the field from the present tenant at a rental of £20 a year, and stating that if the application be not granted then that he may have the use of the Field from 25 March to July next so as to enable him to obtain one elsewhere....And after a lengthy discussion it was moved....that a Committee....be appointed to take charge of and manage the Field with power to recommend arrangements for the letting thereof. (23 November 1898) [12]

Figure 23 The Reverend J B Slight, Rector of Moreton in Essex

A recommendation by the Walks Sub-committee to lease the Walks Field to the Reverend W Boyce was agreed at a meeting of the Property Committee on 22 December, subject to the right of the Corporation to use the Field for any show, exhibition or other public entertainment when required and without any payment. [13] A further letter from the Head Master is recorded in the minutes of the Property Committee but no decision concerning the matter has been found:

> Read a letter of the 7th instant from the Head Master of the Grammar School accepting the offer of the Walks Field opposite the Red Mount for football and cricket on everyday in the week, except Saturdays during the football season, from Lady Day 1899 to Lady Day 1900, subject to the usual conditions, at a rent of £20 per annum, and stating should the British School (Football Club) not come to terms with the Corporation he would be glad to hire the field for the Saturdays during the football season at a rent of £6 per year. And it was agreed that the latter part of the letter be referred to the Walks Field Sub-committee for consideration. (23 February 1899) [14]

The life of the Grammar School under Mr Boyce is described in some detail in my earlier book.[15] Without doubt the most important development during his time as Head Master was the provision of a new building paid for by a former student, William Lancaster (Figure 25). He had left school in 1858 and been taken on as a clerk at the Prudential Assurance Company in London. By 1879, when he was 38, he had become Company Secretary and in 1900 was appointed a Director, the same year as he was invited to become a Governor at his old school. Two years earlier he had endowed a leaving Exhibition, the Lancaster Exhibition worth £30 per year and tenable at any

Figure 24 The Reverend W Boyce, Head Master 1887 to 1919

institution of university, professional or technical instruction approved by the governors. Mr Lancaster was well aware of the deficiencies of the building in St James Street. He is reported to have said that the old school 'was in an entirely unsatisfactory physical condition. It was like the Irishman's coat – hardly a piece of the original garment was left.' It had 'a miserable little playground, not even tar paved as they insist on in the elementary schools in London' and the sanitary arrangements 'were not materially altered since he was there.' Had it 'been an elementary School in London it would have been shut up years ago.' [16] Being by this time a very wealthy man, he decided he would build a new school.

As we saw in the last chapter other former scholars agreed that the buildings were far from satisfactory and this was confirmed by R O Chapman, a boy at the old Lynn Grammar School (Figure 26) from 1904 to 1906, who described the school room as a depressing place:

From the windows nothing could be seen but

other dingy brick buildings in the surrounding back streets, while the scheme of interior decoration (if such drabness could be called decoration) could hardly be described as bright. This place was our sitting room, parlour, common room, or whatever you choose to call it, and after school hours there was nowhere else to go except the very prison-like schoolyard. Most extraordinary of anything were the desks....These venerable things, cumbersome and weighty, were a dozen or fifteen feet in length with very narrow seats attached; positively black with age and possessing lids (under which books were stowed) constantly in a state of disrepair. Almost every square inch of their surface had been cut with initials and names of generations of boys. [17]

Mr Lancaster's proposal to build a new school was set out in a letter to the Mayor in 1902. He stipulated only that the Corporation would provide a suitable site and that the Technical School, opened in 1894 in Hospital Walk, would be merged with the Grammar School:

Figure 25 Sir William Lancaster

The following letter was read from Mr W J Lancaster:

South Lynn
Putney Hill, London
25th February 1902

To his Worshipful the Mayor of King's Lynn

Dear Mr Mayor

The present position of Secondary Education for boys in Lynn is I venture to think not quite so satisfactory as many would wish to see it and so far as I am able to judge I feel that the town is not sufficiently large to support two secondary schools, the Grammar School and the Technical School, successfully.

It has occurred to me that if these two schools could be fused by one of the schemes which has been successfully promoted in other places a great deal of strength that is now weakened by division could be concentrated and we might have one strong school in place of the two which to a certain extent overlap and so weaken each other.

In order that I might be on safe ground before submitting my proposal to the Corporation I interviewed the two official bodies which would have to be consulted upon any such change, the Charity Commissioners and the Board of Education, and I am glad to say that they would both cordially welcome such a proposal and would readily assist in the promotion of any scheme for fusing the two schools. Of course I made it quite clear to them that I called solely in my private capacity.

The Grammar School buildings are old, badly situated, not in the best state of repair, and quite out of accord with modern notions of what school buildings should be. The Corporation I believe possesses a good deal of vacant land in the Borough and the proposal I would ask you to submit to them is this:

If the Corporation will promote and carry through a scheme for the fusing of the two schools under one management and will grant a suitable site, I will undertake to build and present to the Town a new Grammar School upon plans to be approved by them.

The consent of Norfolk County Council would of course be necessary but I have reason to believe that they would consider the question favourably.

I am, dear Mr Mayor
Yours very truly,
W J Lancaster

It was….unanimously resolved that the heartiest thanks of this Council be tendered by the Mayor to Mr W J Lancaster for his munificent offer….And it was resolved that a Committee consisting of eight members of the Hall be appointed to consider the whole question of Mr Lancaster's offer and report to a future meeting and that members of the Town Council on the Technical Education Committee form the Committee. (12 March 1902) [18]

The eventual site for the new building on the Gaywood Road was not initially the first choice, but a site on the (Greyfriars) Tower Field opposite the existing building in St James Street:

On the adoption of the Minutes of the Meeting of the 5th May of the Technical Education Committee, the following Report of Mr H J Green, Architect, and also a letter from the Board of Education in reference to the new school were read namely:

At the request of the Town Clerk for the Borough of King's Lynn I have seen the Borough Engineer who has measured and surveyed the plot of land known as the Tower Field and beg to report that I am of the opinion it is a suitable site for the new school buildings. There are two probable disadvantages to be considered with regard to this site viz.

Figure 26 The Lynn Grammar School in St James Street

1. The space available for a temporary playground would be very limited and
2. Besides covering up an open space in the town it is probable the school buildings would require to be surrounded by a boundary wall and this would to some extent prove a disfigurement to the town.

But against these drawbacks I would point out the following advantages which this spot undoubtedly possess viz.

1. The site is in the centre of the town
2. It is in close proximity to the station
3. If selected no doubt the playing fields on the Walks would be given up as a recreation (area) for the school.
4. The site affords good facilities for drainage

I understand that the proposed building will afford accommodation for 50 resident boarders and 150 day scholars (200 boys in all). (14 May 1902) [19]

Even the architect chosen by William Lancaster seems to have been in favour of the proposed site as shown in a short letter read at a meeting in July 1902:

The following letter from Basil Champneys, the architect engaged by Mr W J Lancaster, as to the proposed site for the new secondary school was read:

> 19 Buckingham Street, Strand
> London, 10th June 1902

Dear Sir

In case my opinion as to the available sites for the proposed new Grammar school is likely to be of service to the Town Council I write to say that, having inspected all the possible positions which I understand to be under consideration, I am decidedly of the opinion that that known as the Tower site is greatly preferable to the others and that I sincerely hope that it may be assigned for the purpose. As I have only just heard that the Meeting of the Town Council is fixed for tomorrow I have not time to give my reasons in detail. I am preparing a report for Mr Lancaster which no doubt will be forwarded to the Council in due course but under the circumstances I may so far anticipate it as to express briefly my very decided opinion on the subject.

> I have the honour to be
> Your faithful servant
> Basil Champneys

The Worshipful
The Mayor of Lynn

Resolved....that the Tower Field be appropriated for the purpose of the new school, subject to the scheme to be formulated, therefore being agreed to by the Corporation. (9 July 1902) [20]

Fortunately, with the benefit of hindsight, there was a great deal of opposition to the use of the Tower Field for the new school:

A resolution passed at a recent meeting of the ratepayers held at the Town Hall was read, protesting against the Tower Field being used as a site for the new Grammar School, but no order was made thereon. (13 August 1902) [21]

This debate was continued at the next meeting of the Council in September at which an attempt to have the decision to appropriate the Tower Field rescinded was not carried. A letter from William Lancaster was read to the Hall:

As to the Tower site I should like the Corporation to understand that I do not wish in any way to influence them in their choice. I hope to provide buildings which will not only be calculated to give a fillip to the town as an educational centre by the provision of the most recent requirements that educational authorities approve, but also to hand them over a school which shall be an architectural ornament to Lynn. If they decide to place it in an outlying district I shall bow to their decision however much I may regret it.

I am writing away from my papers but I feel pretty certain I stipulated a 'suitable site' and while I am quite willing to narrow this term down to a healthy and roomy site, leaving position to the better judgement of the Corporation, I must reserve my right to judge it in these particulars.

It may perhaps save some discussion if I say at once that upon three sites which I see have been suggested I should absolutely decline to build. They are (a) the old burial ground which however I take it the local Government Board would not permit, (b) the present site of the school which in my time more than 40 years ago was closely shut in and must now be worse in this respect, (c) the land between the Walks and St John's Church which I am old enough to remember was a swamp with a stream running through it and is I think little better now.

I saw Mr Mitcheson last month and I am afraid there is no hope of getting the draft scheme before October. (10 September 1902) [22]

Clearly William Lancaster was getting frustrated by the attempts to change the site but the opposition continued in October when a letter was received from the Managers of the St Margaret's National Schools in King's Lynn, objecting to the erection of the new Grammar School on the Tower Field:

Resolved that the Committee appointed to consider the new school scheme be instructed to receive a deputation from the Managers of the St Margaret's Schools at the proper time. (8 October 1902) [23]

The debate continued and, as a result of serious opposition, the decision was taken in February of the following year to abandon plans to build on the Tower Field and instead to open negotiations with the King's Lynn Charity Trustees about acquiring some land on the Gaywood Road to the east of the Almshouses:

The [Education Advisory] Committee considered the question of the site of the proposed new secondary school and it was resolved: That the Town Clerk enter into negotiations with the owners with a view to the acquisition on lease or otherwise of the building land between the Gaywood Almshouses and the Railway Crossing, as the site of the new school.

The Committee carefully considered the draft Scheme for the proposed new secondary school and various amendments were made thereon. (5 February 1903) [24]

After some negotiations the Gaywood Road site was acquired from the Municipal Charity Trustees on a 999 year lease:

A letter was read from Mr E M Beloe, the Clerk to the Charity Trustees….making an offer of the site (as proposed in the Minutes of 5th February) to the Corporation for 999 years, at an annual rental of £100 (23 February 1903) [25]

At the above meeting the Town Clerk reported that he had spoken to Mr Beloe and made a provisional offer of £80 per year and he was authorised to make that offer formally. Following negotiations he brought back a compromise which was accepted:

The Town Clerk submitted [the] resolution passed by the Charity Trustees on the 27th ultimo, offering to lease to the Corporation the Hospital land east of the Gaywood Almshouses for 999 years, at a rent of £90 per year, with the exception of land adjoining the Almshouses to the east and measuring 25 feet in breadth on the line A to B on the plan, the costs of the Clerk and solicitor to the Trustees to be paid by the Corporation.

Resolved: that the Council be recommended to accept the offer, and that the question of costs be left in the hands of the Town Clerk. (11 March 1903) [26]

Mr Lancaster's views on the Gaywood Road site are not recorded but he obviously accepted the decision and it proved to be an excellent one since there was far more room for expansion than would have been possible near the town centre. Some 7.5 acres of land were leased from the Charity Trustees. (This most northerly section of the present-day site extends approximately as far south as the entry to the Art/Technology building.) An additional piece of land (6.122 acres) was leased from the Bagge family in 1905 and bought in 1912, a further piece (4.127 acres) was bought in 1921 and a final section (1.44 acres) in 1966. The freehold on the original parcel of land was bought from the Municipal Charity Trustees by Norfolk County Council in 1965 for £1800.

As a the result of William Lancaster's offer, and the Corporation's acceptance of it, the Grammar School transferred from St James Street to the magnificent building (Figure 27) designed by Basil Champneys. The new building was officially opened by His Majesty King Edward VII on 6 November 1906 and William Lancaster was knighted for his benevolence to the town. At that time the school had only 136 pupils. By the time Mr Boyce retired in 1919 there were 250 on roll and it was a highly-regarded Grammar School. Over the following decades the school continued to grow: in the period after the Second World War there were over 400 pupils; by the mid 1960s, still a boys' grammar school with boarders, it had over 600 on roll; and in the 21st century it is a very successful comprehensive school for over 1300 boys and girls. But this data refers to a school with a different name. In 1903 the Lynn Grammar School and the Technical School were amalgamated, as stipulated by William Lancaster, and the new school's name became King Edward VII Grammar School.

This seems an appropriate point at which to end the diary since the school's subsequent history has been chronicled elsewhere.

Figure 27 King Edward VII Grammar School

Appendix 1.
Charnel Priests and Masters 1511 to 1919

Charnel Priests

Rix	Thomas	1511
Pokering	Thomas	1513
Thorpe	John	1524
Leyton	William	1534
Hall	Richard	1538
Person	Thomas	1538

Schoolmasters

Rackster	John		1550 - 1570
Johnson	Ralph		1570 - 1571
Iverye	John	MA	1571 - 1590 died
Roberts	Alexander	MA	1591 - 1594
Eston	Nicholas	MA	1594 - 1597
Man	John	MA	1597 - 1609
Allston	Henry	MA	1609 - 1612
Armitage	Mr		1612 - 1618 died
Robinson	Robert	BA	1619 - 1625 died
Fishe	Ambrose	MA	1626 - 1627
Woodmansea	Robert	MA	1627 - 1635
Rawlinson	John	MA	1635 - 1637
Bell	Edward	MA	1637 - 1678
Horne	John	MA	1678 - 1730
Squire(s), Revd	Charles	MA	1730 - 1739
Pigge, Revd	Thomas	MA	1739 - 1746
Daville, Revd	John	BA	1746 - 1755
Knox	John		1755 - 1760
Lloyd	David	MA, DCL	1760 - 1794 died
Lloyd, Revd	Henry	MA, BD	1794 - 1797
Scott, Revd	Richard	MA	1797 - 1803
Couchler, Revd	Martin	MA	1803 - 1818 died
Kidd, Revd	Thomas	MA	1818 - 1825
Bransby, Revd	John	MA	1825 - 1850
Bagge Scott, Revd	Francis	MA	1851 - 1858 died
White, Revd	Thomas	MA, LLD	1858 - 1874
Slight, Revd	John	MA	1874 - 1887
Boyce, Revd	Walter	MA	1887 - 1919

Notes:
1. It has not been possible to verify all qualifications.
2. Despite the fact that the Hall Book refers to Mr Armitage as being of Emmanuel College, he is not listed in the *Alumni Cantabrigienses*. Neither has it been possible to locate Messrs John Rackster, Ralph Johnson, John Knox, David Lloyd or Richard Scott in lists of Oxford or Cambridge alumni.

Appendix 2. Grammar School Ushers 1561 to 1758

Downes	Robert	MA	1561 -
Grante	Edward	BA	1568 - 1570
Pollard	Mr	MA	1570 -
Gibson, clerk	John	BA	1571 - 1588
Emott	Richard	BA	1588 -
Man	John	BA	1594 - 1597
Royston/Rosthorn	Henry	MA	1597 - 1602
Foster	Michael	BA	1602 - 1603
Shewte	Robert	MA	1604 - 1607
Emott	Michael	MA	1608 - 1612
Claybrook	Mr		1612 - 1613
Laborne	Edward	MA	1613 - 1642 (died)
Orme	Richard	MA	1642 - 1648
Keene	Edmund	MA	1648 - 1651
Leeds	Edward	MA	1652 - 1659
Gibson	John	BA	1659 - 1661
Kitchingman	John	MA	1661 - 1664
Hayes	James	MA	1664 - 1670
Nesling	Richard	MA	1670 - 1673
Foster	Mark	BA	1674 - 1675
Frost	Thomas	BA	1675 - 1675 (died)
Strutt	Robert	MA	1675 - 1676
Whiting	Joseph	BA	1677 - 1682
Scott	Clement	MA	1682 - 1686
Sheringham	John	MA	1686 - 1688 (died)
Franklin	John	BA	1689 - 1689
Britiffe	Philip	BA	1689 - 1715
Woodyear	Richard	BA	1716 - 1718
Tiffen	William	BA	1718 - 1730
Paine, Revd	Robert	MA	1731 - 1738
Wood, Revd	John	MA	1738 - 1742
Phelps, Revd	Charles	BA	1742 - 1742
Rushbrook, Revd	Robert	BA	1742 - 1746
Hutchinson, Revd	Thomas	BA	1748 - 1755
Birkes	John		1756 - 1758
Aram	Eugene		1758 - 1758

Notes:
1. Degrees are given as listed in the Hall Books or from the *Alumni Cantabrigienses*.
2. In some cases MAs were obtained after leaving the Grammar School.
3. It has not been possible to verify all dates from the Hall Books or Chamberlains' Accounts.

Appendix 3. The Rules of the Grammar School

In the Year 1662 again confirmed

Of Piety

1. Let all the scholars at half-past six in the morning, with bended knees and the rest of the body devoutly disposed, offer prayers to God. Let them do the same at five in the evening.

2. Let the Master admonish those who come not before prayers or behave themselves irreverently during prayers, but let him do it with pious moderation.

3. Let those who are present at Church on feast days and other appointed times in their seats for public prayers hear attentively and devoutly the sermons and whatever lessons may be read from scriptures.

4. Let those who in church behave themselves immodestly or irreverently be punished for such offence.

5. Let them learn the Articles of Faith, the Decalogue, the Lord's Prayer and other things profitable for the faith of a Christian, as well in English as in Latin; and let the Master instruct them upon some of these every Saturday afternoon.

6. Let those who are sufficiently apt at learning and of proper age prepare Declamations in writing, and let them be shown to the Master and let the best of them be delivered.

Of Letters

7. Let the whole School be divided into six classes and forms, the Master moderator to the first three, and the Usher to the rest.

8. Let those who are in the first class, and seem to be fit, learn from the Master the elements of Hebrew, Homer, Sophocles, select orations of Demosthenes and Cicero, the Aeneids of Virgil, the poems of Claudian, the History of Sallust, Quintus Curtius, Suetonius on the Twelve Caesars, the Epitome of Lucius Florus, and Sleidon's little book on the Four Greatest Empires; and let the Master every Saturday instruct them from Nonnus's Paraphrase of St. John's Gospel.

9. The next class, Cicero's Offices, Caesar's Commentaries, Justinian, Hesiod, Theognis, the poems of Horace, Xenophon on Cyrius, and some of the orations of Socrates, and every Saturday the Greek Testament and David's Psalms; and let the Master explain Tale's Rhetoric to those competent.

10. To the third class, Cicero's De Senectute et Amicitia, the chaster comedies of Plautus and Terence, Virgil's Georgics, Ovid's De Tristibus et Ponte, the rudiments of the Greek language, and let them be exercised diligently in the different dialects.

11. Let the fourth form translate the Colloquies of Erasmus, Aesop's Fables, the Select Epistles of Cicero and Virgil's Eclogues.

12. Let the fifth class diligently study the Distiches of Cato, Mancinius on the Virtues, the Colloquies of Corderius, together with Lilly's Rules of Grammar.

13. Let the boys of the last form be studiously exercised in committing to memory the first rules of Grammar.

Of Manners

14. Let him who either in church or in public does not conduct himself modestly be punished.

15. Let all brawling, fighting, noise, pilfering, obscenity and oaths be punished.

16. In the streets, where magistrates, men of years or notability may be, let the head be uncovered and the

way given to them, and let the Master reprove those who neglect to do so.

17. Let no one come to the school with uncombed head, face or hands unwashed, dirty shoes and hose torn, or slovenly dress.

18. Let all the scholars entirely abstain from cards, dice and drink. Let all barbarous writers and obscene poets, whereby morals and purity of the Latin language may be corrupted, be prohibited.

Of Order

19. Let the Masters be pious and good men, diligently teaching the school. Let them inculcate piety and good manners with learning. Let them neither undertake public business nor private employments which may impede their diligence in instruction. Let them not condemn with too much asperity nor change to clemency with too great facility. Let them demand no greater stipend than shall be publically fixed by the Governors. If anything, however, by way of remuneration be voluntarily bestowed, let them accept it without deceit. Let rich and poor have the same consideration; let it be exhibited in teaching and everything else without distinction. Let them never be absent without having good and sufficient deputies substituted for them, who can understand and regard the teacher's office.

20. Let the Usher come to the school at six in the morning and let him diligently employ himself teaching till eleven.

21. Let the Master be there at seven, and depart not till half-past ten. Let both return again at one and spend the time till five in instructing, reading to, and forming the manners of the boys.

22. Let the pupils come at six, and at one from dinner, and let them go to dinner at eleven and to supper at five.

23. Let all who are ignorant of reading and writing be excluded from the school.

24. Let ink, paper, knives, and school books, and also paper books for writing what shall be ordered by the Master, be furnished.

25. Let not those who are being instructed in the first elements of Grammar be giddily confused and like parrots without understanding, but let them say their lessons in an agreeable tone and with apt and just modulation.

26. Let the Masters arrange the course of study neither all at once nor confusedly, but leisurely, illustrating extensively with examples. Let them never go on to new lessons unless the former are known, and fully understood. For it is not important how quickly but how well; nor does it profit to read many things, rather to understand what is read.

27. Let everyone leave this school after six years, either for the University or for further study or for business.

28. Let the loiterer, the dull, the idle, the blockhead, and those who are slow in capacity and too little apt at learning, after three years, when the Master has with certainty ascertained their capacity and disposition, be sent by the Governors from the school to other business for which they are fit.

29. Let the Master appoint Monitors for all noticeable offences committed publicly in church or street and privately in the school. Let the matter be enquired into in five days and the delinquents punished.

30. Let any who were absent in the morning explain in the afternoon to the Master; if in the afternoon, let the cause be explained the following morning.

31. Four times or at least twice a year let the scholars be examined, and let it be faithfully reported what progress has been made.

32. Forasmuch as the powers as well of our minds as of our bodies are not only limited but also weak, for relief thereof let the Master give the scholars permission every Thursday afternoon after two for play and exercise, nevertheless upon condition that the games are of a sort which have innocence combined with enjoyment.

Source: Harrod (1874) and printed in *The Lennensian* No. LXX, Autumn Term 1930.

Appendix 4. Scholarships and Awards to Cambridge

Titley Scholarships to Emmanuel College, Cambridge

John Daynes	(27 Oct 1606, 3 and 10 Feb 1607)
Thomas Robinson	(3 and 10 Feb 1606)
Maurice White	(3 Nov and 8 Dec 1609)
Bartholomew Adrian	(18 Feb 1611) in the place of John Daynes
Thomas Halliday	(18 March 1614 and 7 July 1615).
Thomas Bolton	(29 May and 25 Sept 1618) in the place of Bart. Adrian
John Ewer	(17 Jan and 20 Mar 1619) in the place of Thomas Halliday
Thomas Walker	(3 and 11 Oct 1623) in the place of John Ewer
Richard More	(26 May and 14 July 1626) in the place of Thomas Bolton
Thomas Leech	(9 July 1630 and 17 Jan 1631) in the place of Richard More
William Gurnall	(2 Dec 1631) in the place of Thomas Walker
John Maxie	(26 Feb 1638). No university record found.
Thomas Theoderick	(4 Feb and 18 Mar 1639)
Hampden Reeve	(21 June 1639) in the place of William Gurnall
Benedict Riveley	(29 Aug and 27 Sept 1644)
William Williams	(16 March 1646)
Luke Eales	(17 Nov and 5 Dec 1651) in the place of Benedict Riveley
Michael Stukeley	(4 and 15 April 1653)
Thomas Dix	(18 and 25 April 1659) in the place of Luke Eales
James Hayes	(22 and 25 Feb 1661) in the place of Michael Stukely
John May	(25 Dec 1662) in the place of Thomas Dix (deceased)
Richard Nesling	(3 March 1665) in the place of James Hayes
Nathaniel Osborne	(29 Jan 1669) in the place of John May.
William Needham	(17 March 1671)
Nathaniel Ferrier	(2 and 9 March 1677)
Gervaise Needham	(14 June and 29 July 1678)
Edward Francis	(14 June and 29 July 1678)
Robert Butler	(20 Jan 1679) in the place of Edward Francis
Matthew Scott	(26 Oct and 6 Nov 1691) in the place of Gervaise Needham.
Phillip Franklyn	admitted 1687 (no Hall Book record found). Died 1689
William Houghton	(15 and 29 Aug 1692) in the place of Phillip Franklyn
Charles Phelps	(9 Sept 1731)
Thomas Stona	(29 Sept 1744)
John Fairfax Franklin	(9 Jan 1760)
Henry Smith	(4 Sept 1771)
William Hardyman	(29 Sept 1781)
Charles Lloyd	(5 June 1795) in the place of Henry Smith
William Bedel Coulcher[*1]	(14 Feb 1818).
John Raven	(14 Feb 1818)
Richard Bentley Porson Kidd[*2]	(13 Feb 1826)
William Begley	(1829). No record found of confirmation by Corporation.

Thomas Parlett Platten	(31 Dec 1830)
John William Greaves	(13 March 1833) in the place of RBP Kidd

[*1] Son of the Master of the Grammar School, the Revd. Martin Coulcher.
[*2] Son of the Master of the Grammar School, the Revd. Thomas Kidd.

John Peirson's Award

John Fawcett	Christ's College (14 Jan and 8 July 1625)
Thomas Walker	Emmanuel (5 May 1628) from Michaelmas 1628
Thomas Leech	Emmanuel (29 March 1633)
John Maxie	(26 Feb 1638). No university record found.
Thomas Theoderick	Emmanuel (21 June 1639)
Edward Bradford	No Hall Book nor university records found.
Benedict Riveley	Emmanuel (16 Dec 1644) in the place of Edward Bradford
Thomas Thurlin	St John's College (18 Sept 1651) in the place of B Riveley
Edward Tilson	Christ's College (23 March 1657) in the place of T Thurlin
Joshua Bassett	Caius College (17 October 1659) in the place of Edward Tilson, (deceased)
William Needham	Emmanuel (31 March 1671) in the place of Richard Nesling
Gervaise Needham	Emmanuel (14 June 1678) in the place of W Needham.
Edward Hart	Christ's College (27 May 1692)
Robert Rolfe	Caius College (5 Nov 1739)
George William Lemon	Queens' College (29 Set 1744)
Henry Lloyd[*3]	Trinity College (29 Sept 1781)
William Johnson	St John's College (29 Sep 1787)
Stephen Allen	Trinity College (11 Sept 1793)
Hamnett Holditch	Caius College (14 Feb 1818)
George Coulcher	Corpus Christi College (14 Feb 1827)
Alfred Legge	Peterhouse (19 Nov 1862)

[*3] Son of the Master of the Grammar School, Dr David Lloyd.

Alexander Hall's Award

Thomas Thurlin	St John's College (18 Sept 1651)
Edward Tilson	Christ's College (23 March 1657) in the place of T Thurlin
Joshua Bassett	Caius College (17 Oct 1659) in the place of Edward Tilson, deceased
John Gedney	Corpus Christi College, 1667 (no Hall book entry found)
Nathaniel Osborne	Emmanuel (31 March 1671) in the place of John Gedney
Robert Walwin	(no Hall Book entry found)
Benjamin Keene	(14 Oct 1687) in the place of Robert Walwin, deceased
Edward Hart	Christ's College (27 May 1692)
William Scott	Trinity College (29 Nov 1742)
Henry Lloyd	Trinity College (29 Sep 1781)
Hamnett Holditch	Caius College (14 Feb 1818)
William Hunter Bennell	St John's College (11 May 1885)
Ernest Edward Hitchcock	Cavendish House (11 May 1885)

Thomas Thurlin Exhibitions to St John's College, Cambridge

Henry Michelson	(3 Feb 1736)
John Cott	(16 Dec 1745)
Thomas Wetherhead	(29 May 1761)
Thomas Catton	(4 June 1779)
William Johnson	(14 Feb 1787)
Philip Pratt	(29 Aug 1797)
Thomas William Greaves	(13 June 1825)
Robert Carr	(6 Nov 1848). See note 3.
Thomas Oldmeadow Price	(19 Nov 1862)

Notes:

1. The dates refer to entries in the Hall Books when the scholar was nominated and/or the scholarship/ award was confirmed by the Corporation.

2. These lists are almost certainly not complete. Not all references to awards have been located in the Hall Books as shown by the fact that some names are mentioned when a new award has been made but the award to the previous holder is missing. In addition the Municipal Corporations Act of 1835 transferred the management of charitable funds which had been administered by the unreformed corporations to bodies of municipal charities. So for a period of about 50 years the Trustees of the King's Lynn Municipal Charities acted as custodians of the Titley, Peirson and Thurlin funds, but no records of any awards made by them have survived.

3. The entry in the Hall Book (6 Nov. 1848) orders that the application by Robert Carr for the Thurlin Exhibition should be referred to the Charity Trustees. He was admitted to St John's in 1848 but there is no record of him gaining a degree.

References

Introduction

1. Cheney, C R, *A Handbook of Dates – for students of British History*, Cambridge University Press, 2nd Edition, 2000
2. www.measuringworth.com

Chapter 1

1. Eller, G, *Memorials, Archaeological and Ecclesiastical of the West Winch Manors*, King's Lynn, 1861
2. Hall Book 3, (KL/C7/5) page 99
3. op. cit. page 110
4. op. cit. page 136,
5. op. cit. page 246d,
6. op. cit. page 294d,
7. op. cit. page 315d
8. op. cit. page 317d
9. KL/C58/2/1
10. KL/C58/34
11. Sykes, P, *King's Lynn Town Surveys*, 1568-1589, King's Lynn, 2000
12. KL/C10/20
13. Parkin, C, *The topography of Freebridge Hundred and Half in the county of Norfolk, containing the history and antiquities of King's Lynn*, King's Lynn, 1762
14. KL/C58/24
15. KL/C58/26
16. KL/C58/24
17. KL/C58/18
18. *The Report of a Commission Inquiring into Public Charities*, J W Atkin, King's Lynn, 1843

Chapter 2

1. Hall Book 4, (KL/C7/6) page 140
2. op.cit. page 94
3. op.cit. page 150
4. op.cit. page 196
5. op.cit. page 230
6. op.cit. page 242
7. op.cit. page 365
8. op.cit. page 497
9. Hall Book 5, (KL/C7/7) page 14
10. op.cit. page 47
11. op.cit. page 191
12. op.cit. page 208
13. op.cit. page 248
14. Parker, V, *The Making of King's Lynn*, Phillimore, Chichester, 1971
15. Hall Book 5, (KL/C7/7) page 362
16. op.cit. page 374
17. op.cit. page 376
18. op.cit. page 407
19. op.cit. page 421
20. Hall Book 6, (KL/C7/8) page 43
21. op.cit. page 82
22. op.cit. page 252
23. op.cit. page 283
24. op.cit. page 360
25. op.cit. page 374
26. KL/C58/11
27. Harrod, H, *Report on the Deeds and Records of the Borough of Lynn*, Thew & Son, King's Lynn, 1874
28. Hall Book 6, (KL/C7/8) page 430
29. op.cit. page 446
30. op.cit. page 465
31. Hall Book 7, (KL/C7/9) page 21
32. op.cit. page 24
33. op.cit. page 25
34. op.cit. page 44
35. op.cit. page 28
36. op.cit. page 117
37. op.cit. page 139
38. op.cit. page 261
39. op.cit. page 137a
40. op.cit. page 251
41. Hall Book 8, (KL/C7/10) page 357
42. Hall Book 7, (KL/C7/9) page 408
43. op.cit. page 276
44. op.cit. page 409
45. Chamberlains' Accounts, 1599-1600, (KL/C39/97) page 29
46. www.littlewoodham.org.uk/research/mark.htm
47. Hall Book 7, (KL/C7/9) page 418

Chapter 3

1. Hall Book 6 (KL/C7/8), page 294
2. op.cit. pages 379 to 380
3. op.cit. page 389
4. op.cit. page 440
5. Hall Book 7 (KL/C7/9), page 47
6. Hall Book 6 (KL/C7/8), page 477
7. op.cit. page 482
8. Hall Book 7 (KL/C7/9), page 129
9. op.cit. page 212
10. op.cit. page 255
11. Hall Book 8 (KL/C7/10), page 44
12. op.cit. page 51
13. Venn, J and J A, *Alumni Cantabrigienses.* (Up to 1751,1922-27 and 1752 to 1900, 1940 -1954), reprinted, Theommes Press, Bristol, 2001
14. Hall Book 7 (KL/C7/9), page 237
15. op.cit. page 230
16. op.cit. page 237
17. op.cit. page 345
18. Hall Book 8 (KL/C7/10), page 321
19. op.cit. page 513
20. Hall Book 9, (KL/C7/11), page 70
21. op.cit. page 178
22. Hall Book 11, (KL/C7/13), page 101
23. op.cit. page 150
24. op.cit. page 345
25. op.cit. page 376
26. op.cit. page 57

27 Hall Book 12, (KL/C7/14), page 270.

28 op.cit. page 352

29 Hall Book 13, (KL/C7/15), page 113

Chapter 4

1 Hall Book 7 (KL/C7/9), page 470

2 Hall Book 8 (KL/C7/10), page 4

3 Source: Blomefield, F, *An Essay towards a topographical History of the County of Norfolk.* (Vol. 8 by Parkin, C), London, 2nd Edition, 1808. (Map re-engraved by B Howlett)

4 Hall Book 8 (KL/C7/10), page 31

5 op.cit. page 390

6 op.cit. page 391

7 Higgins, D, *Mr Henry Bell*, Phoenix Publications, King's Lynn, 2005

8 Hall Book 9 (KL/C7/11), page 13

9 Hall Book 8 (KL/C7/10), page 86

10 op.cit. page 90

11 op.cit. page 250

12 op.cit. page 305

13 Hall Book 9 (KL/C7/11), page 24

14 op.cit. page 293

15 op.cit. page 359

16 op.cit. page 19

17 op.cit. page 119

18 op.cit. page 444

19 op.cit. page 436

20 op.cit. page 444

21 op.cit. page 451

22 op.cit. page 464

23 Vernon, L C, 'The History of the School through Four Centuries' in *The Lennesian*, Michaelmas 1931)

24 Hall Book 10 (KL/C7/12), page 51

25 Hall Book 9 (KL/C7/11), page 495

26 Hall Book 10 (KL/C7/12), page 84

27 op.cit. page 362

28 op.cit. page 517

29 op.cit. page 520

Chapter 5

1 Hall Book 10 (KL/C7/12), page 521

2 op.cit. page 529

3 Hall Book 11 (KL/C7/13), page 11

4 Mackerell, B, *The History and Antiquities of the Flourishing Corporation of King's Lynn*, London, 1738

5 Hall Book 11 (KL/C7/13), page 82

6 op.cit. page 85

7 op.cit. page 166

8 op.cit. page 167

9 op.cit. page 169

10 KL/C58/13

11 KL/C58/11

12 Hall Book 11 (KL/C7/13), page 179

13 op.cit. page 181

14 op.cit. page 188

15 op.cit. page 194

16 op.cit. page 277

17 op.cit. page 254

18 op.cit. page 314

19 op.cit. page 328

20 op.cit. page 344

21 op.cit. page 378

22 Dobson, J, 'The College Criminals: 2. Eugene Aram', in *The Annals of the Royal College of Surgeons of England*, Volume 10, April 1952.

23 op.cit. page 389

24 op.cit. page 420

25 op.cit. page 424

26 op.cit. page 428

Chapter 6

1 Taylor, W, *The Antiquities of King's Lynn, Norfolk*, King's Lynn, 1844.

2 Source: Higgins, D, *Mr Henry Bell*, Phoenix Publications, 2005

3 Beloe, E M, *Our Borough: Our Churches*, Macmillan and Bowes, 1899

4 Hall Book 12, (KL/C7/14), pages 18-19

5 op.cit. page 97

6 op.cit. page 190

7 op.cit. page 191

8 op.cit. page 195

9 op.cit. page 245

10 op.cit. page 326

11 op.cit. page 342

12 op.cit. page 378

13 op.cit. page 392

14 Hall Book 13, (KL/C7/15), page 134

15 KL/C58/16

16 Hall Book 13, (KL/C7/15), page 372

17 op.cit. page 394

18 Hall Book 14, (KL/C7/16), page 87

19 Hall Book 13, (KL/C7/15), page 411

20 op.cit. page 415

21 Hall Book 14, (KL/C7/16), page 16

Chapter 7

1 Hall Book 14 (KL/C7/16), pages 67/68

2 op.cit. page 71

3 op.cit. page 74

4 op.cit. page 77

5 Committee Book 2 (KL/TC2/1/2), page 84

6 Hall Book 14 (KL/C7/16), page 174

7 Venn, J and J A, *Alumni Cantabrigienses.* (to 1751,1922-27 and 1752 to

1900, 1940 -1954), reprinted, Theommes Press, Bristol, 2001

8 Hall Book 14 (KL/C7/16), page 206

9 op.cit. page 256

10 op.cit. page 325

11 KL/C10/20

12 Hall Book 14 (KL/C7/16), page 329

13 Committee Book 3 (KL/TC2/1/3), pages 18/21

14 Hall Book 14 (KL/C7/16), page 332

15 op.cit. page 334

16 KL/C10/20

17 Hall Book 14 (KL/C7/16), page 342

18 KL/58/26

19 op.cit

20 Hall Book 14 (KL/C7/16), page 397

21 op.cit. page 424

22 op.cit. page 436

23 KL/58/26

24 op.cit.

25 Hall Book 14 (KL/C7/16), page 530

26 Committee Book 3 (KL/TC2/1/3), pages 150/1

27 Hall Book 14 (KL/C7/16), page 612

28 Committee Book 3 (KL/TC2/1/3), page 396

29 op.cit. page 398

30 op.cit. page 399

Chapter 8

1 Hall Book 15 (KL/C7/17-18), pages 130-131

2 op.cit. page 230

3 op.cit. page 247

4 Committee Book 4 (KL/TC2/1/4), page 208

5 Hall Book 15 (KL/C7/17-18), page 476

6 op.cit. pages 516-517

7 op.cit. 519-520

8 Committee Book 5

(KL/TC2/1/5), page 169

9 Hall Book 15 (KL/C7/17-18), page 553

10 Committee Book 5, (KL/TC2/1/5), pages 232-233

11 Hall Book 15 (KL/C7/17-18), page 754

12 Hall Book 16 (KL/C7/19-20), pages 19/20

13 op.cit. page 57

14 Hall Book 15 (KL/C7/17-18), pages 761/62

15 Hall Book 16 (KL/C7/19-20), pages 24/25

16 Committee Book 6, (KL/TC1/1/6), page 229

17 KL/C58/33

18 Hammond, JL, Royal Schools' Inquiry Commission,1865

19 Hall Book 16 (KL/C7/19-20), pages 41-42

20 Cambridgeshire Herald, 21 April 1866

21 Coulton, G G, *Four Score Years*, Cambridge University Press, 1944

22 Hitchcock, R C, 'Sixty Years Ago', in *The Lennensian*, Winter 1934.

23 Hall Book 16 (KL/C7/19-20), pages 705-706

24 op.cit. pages 707-708

25 op.cit. page 728

26 Committee Book 9, (KL/TC1/1/9), page 245

27 Hall Book 17 (KL/C7/21-22), page 91

28 op.cit. page 108

29 op.cit. page 137

30 op.cit. page 162

31 op.cit. page 399

32 op.cit. page 405

33 op.cit. page 733

34 op.cit. page 800

Chapter 9

1 Hall Book 18 (KL/C7/23-24), page 36

2 op.cit. pages 40-41 and 44

3 op.cit. pages 279-280

4 King's Lynn Grammar School Governors' Minute Book, 1884-1890, 21 October 1886

5 op.cit. 20 April 1887

6 op.cit. 11 May 1887

7 op.cit. 23 May 1887

8 op.cit. 7 June 1887

9 op.cit. 28 June 1887

10 op.cit. 11 July 1887

11 Hall Book 18 (KL/C7/23-24), page 229

12 Committee Book 16 (KL/TC1/1/16) page153

13 op.cit. pages 178-179

14 op.cit. pages 206-207

15 Walker, M, *King Edward Vll School, A Centenary Celebration*, Book Guild Publishing, 2005

16 In a speech at the Lunch given by the Corporation following the Official Opening of the new building on 5 November 1906.

17 Chapman, R O, 'Twenty-three Years Ago', in *The Lennensian*, Summer 1927

18 Hall Book 20 (KL/C7/27-28), page 120

19 op.cit. pages 144-145

20 op.cit. pages 156-157

21 op.cit. page 164

22 op.cit. pages 168-169

23 op.cit. page 172

24 Hall Book 21(KL/TC1/1), page 106

25 op.cit. pages 109-110

26 op.cit. page 112

Index